"Hal Cunnyngham and Amanda Dimpe... of steps churches and groups can take to make the Great Commission task their own. The pages of this book contain wisdom produced by more than a decade of consultancies in Asia, Africa, Europe, and the Americas. The results recorded here point to an effective process. Those who work through these *Eight Steps* will empower local churches with the biblical basis for missions and provide the actual steps they need to join the Great Commission task of sending missionaries cross-culturally in a sustainable fashion. These *Eight Steps* provide a clear process for the global church to partner together to put feet to the vision of the whole church owning the mission task."

> — **JOHN BRADY, vice president for global engagement, International Mission Board**

"The missionary task is enormous and complex. *Eight Steps of the Missions Continuum* provides the strategic foundation for every church to participate in the Great Commission. It helps churches understand the urgency of the task and transcends cultural challenges. Although many ethnic groups of the world have been a mission field for a long time, we are grateful for the opportunity for these ethnic churches to now be part of the mission force reaching the world for Christ."

> — **PETER YANES, executive director for Asian American relations and mobilization, SBC Executive Committee**

"I have been in the ministry for 32 years and one of the *Eight Steps* workshops made me reevaluate what I am doing. Is it biblical or just following others' methods? I will never [again] plant a church that doesn't have missions as its ultimate focus."

> — **PALAN RAMASAMY, vice chairman, Malaysian Baptist Convention**

"The *Eight Steps* process is about creating a culture of evangelism, disciple-making, equipping leaders, and sending members as missionaries to reach the nations for the glory of God. Thank you for training us to develop this sending culture in our churches!"

— **RALPH GARAY, international church planting strategist, Baptist State Convention of North Carolina**

"The *Eight Steps* process is interactive, adaptable, informative, and most of all covers valuable content to result in churches and conventions sending missionaries. One thing we all appreciate is a framework we can take and contextualize as we implement it in various countries across Africa."

— **DAREN DAVIS, affinity leader, sub-Saharan Africa, International Mission Board**

Eight Steps
of the
Missions
Continuum

Blessin on your ministry

Eight Steps
of the
Missions
Continuum

*Building a Bridge from the Church
to the Mission Field*

Hal Cunnyngham &
Amanda Dimperio Davis

INTERNATIONAL MISSION BOARD
RICHMOND
2022

Published by the International Mission Board, SBC

P.O. Box 6767

Richmond, Virginia 23230-0767

http://imb.org

Scripture quotations in this work are taken from the Christian
Standard Bible®, Copyright © 2017 by Holman Bible Publishers.
Used by permission. Christian Standard Bible® and CSB® are
federally registered trademarks of Holman Bible Publishers.

ISBN: 978 1 7344 7674 3

Editor: Robin D. Martin
Cover & Text Designer: Edward A. Crawford

*Names and identifying information in this book denoted with
an asterisk have been changed for security reasons.

This book is dedicated to the thousands of cross-cultural workers around the globe, taking the gospel from everywhere to everywhere.

CONTENTS

ACKNOWLEDGMENTS

WE WANT TO THANK AND ACKNOWLEDGE the contributions of many of our International Mission Board colleagues who participated in the development of the cross-cultural missionary assessment portion of the *Eight Steps* process, Step Six. Those early consultations helped reveal many of the challenges sending churches and organizations face as they work to deploy international missionaries. The comprehensive assessment process has proven to be a key ingredient in achieving the goal of sending the right persons to the right places at the right times. Those colleagues include Kelly Davis, Ted Davis, Bob Dilks, Alan Garnett, Larry Gay, Susan Gay, Joel Sutton, and Andy Tuttle.

PREFACE

I T WAS ONE OF THE MOST UNIQUE EVENTS we had ever attended as we gathered in a sprawling Asian city, meeting with partners representing key missions-sending organizations from about twenty different countries. It was 2012 and we had assembled to discuss global missions. Although language and cultural differences abounded, there was a spirit of unity among the participants. That unifying spirit emerged from our understanding of the Great Commission – God's call for churches and believers everywhere to fully embrace the command to "make disciples of all nations."

While the shared vision was uplifting, the consistent challenges these missionaries faced around the world were discouraging. One common issue that rose above the rest was that of missionaries not remaining on their field of service long enough to effectively share the gospel. In fact, the leader of one major missions-sending network shared that the attrition rate for his organization was hovering around 85 percent. When he said this, we thought it was a mistake, that he meant to say only 85 percent were able to complete a minimal one- or two-year term. However, he repeated his original statement. Only about 15 percent of his organization's missionaries were actually able to complete their first term of service.

This statement shocked us and was something we had not anticipated. How could missionaries impact lostness if they could not remain among those who were lost and needed the gospel? We surveyed other representatives attending the conference, and through frank conversation found that this was happening with other senders as well. Simply sustaining missionary presence on the field was a major obstacle, one that participants wanted to discuss once they learned that others had the same overarching challenge. One partner shared that he felt God had uniquely prepared missionaries from his country to go to difficult places because they had suffered from religious persecution in their own home country throughout their lives. Yet, although they had a willingness to suffer for the sake of the gospel, other factors were defeating their missionaries and the high attrition was causing suffering of a different type. This partner asked, "Since you have so many years of experience, can you help us suffer less?" Suffering, to him, was his mission organization's inability to keep missionaries on the field.

The International Mission Board (IMB) is an agency with more than 175 years of experience in sending cross-cultural missionaries. However, hearing the stories of struggles from Christian leaders at this event helped us realize our own blind spots in helping new missions organizations establish their own sending processes. The structures, procedures, and policies from our US-based agency were not transferring adequately to address the needs of the non-North American agencies, or "majority-world" sending organizations. We began to revisit two questions that constantly surfaced in these discussions: How could we truly help these partners establish organizations that would work closely with the local church in their respective countries? And how could we help them sustain missionary presence on the mission field and therefore be effective in engaging lostness and making disciples, as commanded in the Great Commission?

The answers were evasive. Our previous assumptions of simply translating our North American structures, policies, and strategies to their majority-world sending organizations were not helping impact the world's lostness. We needed a new paradigm if we wanted to serve these worldwide partner agencies and churches as they ramp up missions sending.

In seeking an answer, we recognized that if we continued with our traditional approach, our contribution to the effectiveness of majority-world missions sending would be minimal. We had to learn from those we were hoping to serve. So, when the opportunity arose to train international partners in missionary assessment, we began using these training sessions in various parts of the world to listen to these partners. We began hearing their vision and sense of God's calling on their lives. We were also able to identify the circumstances that were bringing their missionaries home and analyze how best to help them move toward more effective and sustainable missions sending.

We also reviewed the struggles our own organization has faced over the years. Throughout its history, the IMB has reorganized its home office and field structures to continually meet the needs of a changing world. Just as the world situation is not stagnant, no organizational structure is permanent. The influences of political upheaval, natural disasters, wars, coups, and pandemics have necessitated change. While we can learn from models of the past, we must more importantly look toward the needs of the future, focusing on how we can best communicate the gospel to unreached peoples and places. Likewise, we must work with our partners to help them analyze where they are, looking to the future with faith in the Lord's provision.

Over the next six years, invitations to work with partners to develop missionary assessment processes took us to Asia, sub-Saharan Africa, South America, and the Middle East. We met with believers in a variety of locations, from the nineteenth floor of a high rise in an Asian megacity, to a bamboo hut on the shore of the Mekong River.

All of these believers were seeking to embrace their role in the Great Commission. While partners expressed a variety of concerns, trends began to emerge as we learned of their challenges. Then, in 2019, at the conclusion of one of these consultation trips, we listed all the challenges we had observed on flip-chart papers taped to the wall of a meeting room. The trends were evident. Most of our observations fell into eight basic areas. We realized that to truly be helpful to global partners we needed to help them analyze their own situation in each of these eight areas, then help them develop plans to grow in the areas they deemed most important to expand their missions-sending capacity. Those areas became the *Eight Steps of the Missions Continuum.* For our partners, the analysis must be their own, but we had a role to help them navigate the process.

The *Eight Steps* are simple. None are unknown concepts to the evangelical community. In fact, the simplicity is the beauty of the *Eight Steps* process. When we conduct an *Eight Steps* consultation, the process unpacks each step to evaluate the current status of a church or sending organization and helps the group develop plans to advance its missionary efforts.

For example, let's revisit the problem of missionaries struggling to remain on the field. Walking through the *Eight Steps* can be helpful in preventing some of these losses. "Raising up Missionaries" (Step Four) outlines Bible studies that can be discussed in community in the local church to help candidates discern if they are called to missions and if they are ready. "Selecting and Training Cross-Cultural Missionaries" (Step Six) covers the five components of missionary assessment, such as the process of identifying the candidate's qualifications and competencies. "Developing Partnerships" (Step Seven) recognizes that small and large churches and agencies alike cannot be experts in all aspects of missions sending and need to partner with others to develop well-rounded processes. Step Eight – "The Mission Field: Defining the Missionary Task" – details what is required within the Missionary Task, and what unique competencies and qualifications are needed in a particular location and for a particular job.

Each of these steps guides a church or organization in sending the right person to the right place at the right time. Using the studies in each of these steps will help the church and missionary candidates engage in a process to answer these questions in community, which is a healthy way to make the best decisions for all: the prospective missionary, the church, the agency, and those on the mission field. Usually, a major deficit in two or three of these steps leads to dysfunction in the sending process and missionaries who are not able to stay on the mission field, and even if they do, they are minimally effective.

In this book we will describe and unpack the concepts behind each of the steps, citing actual case studies from around the world. However, knowledge alone is not enough. We hope to build a foundation of knowledge that can lead to actual change, or transformation as described in Romans 12:1-3: "... be transformed by the renewing of your mind, so that you may discern what is the good, pleasing, and perfect will of God." The case studies illustrating each step will not only highlight the evaluation that took place, but how partners then developed and implemented plans to address their particular challenges and expand their missions-sending capacity. This desired transformation is more likely to take place in the context of community, where like-minded individuals study Scripture, analyze their situation on each of the *Eight Steps,* and agree to develop plans to work together to embrace their calling more fully toward the Great Commission.

There are many books that discuss who is responsible for missions, whether it is the church, believers, or agencies. The answer is that all three are responsible, and all three must work together. Individual believers are a part of the local church. Agencies provide different resources and can fill in the gaps that many churches are not equipped to address. So, the question is not who is responsible. The question is how can we leverage the strengths of all three?

Another unique aspect of this book is where we begin – not with Step One but with Step Eight, the Mission Field and the implementation of the Missionary Task. This is critical to the process. We must know where we are going if we are truly going to build a bridge to get there. The Great Commission depends on the gospel being shared with those who have never heard. Thus, implementing the Missionary Task is critical for any missionary-sending enterprise to fully embrace the Great Commission.

We hope this book motivates you to analyze where you are and to take steps to maximize your own church or organization's involvement in the Great Commission. God gave the commission to all believers and churches, and he will provide the way to fulfill that calling as you earnestly seek him through his Word, prayer, and consultation with other believers.

Let us all be encouraged to embrace the many promises found in God's Word, such as that recorded in 2 Corinthians 9:8 which says: "And God is able to make every grace overflow to you, so that in every way, always having everything you need, you may excel in every good work."

Hal Cunnyngham, Ed.D.
Amanda Dimperio Davis, D.Min.

STEP EIGHT

The Mission Field

Defining the Missionary Task

EXCITEMENT filled the small Texas church as word spread that Mike and Beth Kramer* sensed God's call to serve as overseas missionaries. When the Kramer family shared their news, the missions energy spread throughout the fellowship. The Kramers began their preparations, which included raising funds, securing visas, and packing their family of four, to move overseas. The Kramers had a 7-year-old son, Billy, and a daughter named Christy, 16. Although they understood this overseas move would be a challenge for their children, especially at Christy's age, they saw any delay in following God's call on their lives as disobedience.

Mike and Beth seemed ideal candidates for the missionary effort they were undertaking. Mike had served as an elder in his church while working as a successful salesman in a local business. He shared the gospel effectively in his community, and the Kramers also led a weekly small group Bible study and prayer time in their home. They felt their ministry in the local church had prepared them well for service overseas. Things moved quickly and before many months had passed, the Kramers found themselves adjusting to life in an East Asian city of several million, studying one of the more complex languages in the world — a language completely different from English and the bit of Spanish they had studied in high school.

The excitement of moving overseas quickly waned as the Kramer family began to encounter problems almost immediately upon arrival. Their financial support was on a shoestring budget from the start, but when they arrived overseas, the exchange rate had shifted, making the local currency more expensive. With this exchange-rate fluctuation, they lost almost 20 percent of their buying power. Language study had also presented unanticipated challenges. Beth proved to be an excellent language student and connected well with their language teacher. Mike, however, discovered he had an undiagnosed hearing loss and found it difficult to hear and make the proper sounds in the tonal language they were studying. He had never before been in a situation in which he depended on Beth to communicate. He also found that ministry in this cultural setting was much different than the small group back home. People asked questions that were foreign to his experience — questions related to the worship of ancestors and the fear of the spirit world. At this point in their ministry, Mike and Beth had to work through a translator, and they often wondered if the translator even understood what they were saying.

After only six months on the field, problems continued to mount as their frustration and disappointment grew. The couple began to doubt that the Lord was in this move at all. Perhaps they had misunderstood God's leading. Maybe the members of their church back home had misunderstood as well.

The most critical issue that surfaced during their first six months on the field was concern for the emotional state of their daughter, Christy.

After a few months in their new East Asian home, Christy celebrated her seventeenth birthday and deeply longed for her friends back at her Texas school and church. Although she was a good student and did well in online school courses, she missed the social community of her friends. Without speaking the host language, Christy did not find acceptance with the youth at the local church, no matter how much she tried. Her longing descended into depression and the Kramers grew increasingly worried about Christy and her state of mind. After less than a year on the field, counselors recommended that the family return to the US to treat Christy's depression more adequately.

UNEXPECTED CHALLENGES

MISSIONARIES ENCOUNTERING DIFFICULTIES on the field is nothing new. As a matter of fact, new missionaries should expect frustrations, and most field-orientation programs help families understand many of the challenges they may face. These issues can cause great stress for a cross-cultural missionary family or individual, regardless of where they are from. In the case of Mike and Beth Kramer, attention to several of the *Eight Steps of the Missions Continuum* prior to moving overseas would have helped equip them for the challenges they had to face upon arrival and could possibly have helped them avoid some of the difficulties. The Missionary Task, which is defined in the culminating step of the *Eight Steps of the Missions Continuum*, offers much to consider for prospective missionaries. We will begin by examining this important concept in this first chapter.

An old adage states: "If you don't know where you are going, any road will get you there." At times individuals deploy to a field of service with great anticipation and fervor to be missionaries. Yet they lack understanding as to what they really want and need to do, the pathway to get there, or even how to get started. Too often new missionaries may focus on ministries that may be worthwhile and provide a service to the local community, but that have little impact toward accomplishing the Great Commission. Understanding the Missionary Task, where a missionary wants to go and what he or she needs to do, is critical in order to build the bridge to get there.

Let's look at the Missionary Task in the context of the Kramer's situation. Mike and Beth had excellent ministry experience in their home environment, and they had a thorough understanding of Scripture and how to share their faith in their own culture. However, they had little training related to the components of the Missionary Task, especially the key elements of entry and evangelism. Orientation and training on understanding worldview and cultural context would have helped them to know how to engage others and address their life problems with the Word. Without this foundational understanding, the Kramers were alarmed when they experienced culture shock and a worldview so completely foreign from their own. Likewise, they had no idea of where to begin with sharing the gospel or basic discipleship, much less how to start a church in the foreign culture.

Analysis of many missions-sending endeavors has shown that in too many cases, organizations or churches deploy missionaries to mission fields very different from their own with little or no training in how to identify the context in which they will need to work. The components of the Missionary Task[1] serve as a guide to help missionaries establish and sustain Great Commission strategies among an unreached people or place. Those components are entry, evangelism, discipleship, healthy church formation, leadership development, and exit to partnership, all while abiding in Christ. A study of the Missionary Task can build a clear understanding of what needs to be accomplished and the pathway to get there. Additionally, the Missionary Task components can give missionaries tools to understand the context in which they must work as well as the competencies and qualifications necessary to work in that environment.

Entry. Entry is more than just being physically present. Entry is important to position the missionary for effective cross-cultural ministry. The first element of entry is research: learning about a target population. This can include history, worldview, religions, status of gospel proclamation, availability of Scripture translations (spoken and written), and other pertinent factors such as literacy rates, the economy, and religious persecution in the area. Understanding these various aspects of entry can help the new

1. "The Missionary Task," in *Foundations* (Richmond, VA: IMB, 2018), 75-101.

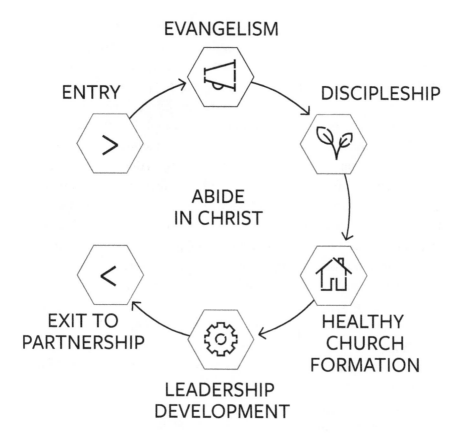

EVANGELISM

ENTRY

DISCIPLESHIP

ABIDE
IN CHRIST

EXIT TO
PARTNERSHIP

HEALTHY
CHURCH
FORMATION

LEADERSHIP
DEVELOPMENT

missionary know where to begin. Had the Kramer family understood the worldview of the host culture they were entering, they could have studied appropriate Scripture passages useful in addressing the issues that quickly surfaced in their evangelism and discipleship situations.

Other aspects of entry are identity and presence. The Kramers were able to live in their city officially as missionaries, but in countries or places where Christian missionaries are not welcome, missionaries must enter with another legitimate reason for being there. Additionally, access to people does not only mean living in their village or city, but also consistently interacting with community members in meaningful ways as they live their lives. Missionaries must be prepared to answer the oft-asked questions: "Who are you?" "What do you do?" and "Why are you here?"

Evangelism. Understanding how to approach the Missionary Task in the local context can be a daunting endeavor. In asking prospective missionaries to define the Missionary Task, most focus on evangelism with their most common response being "sharing the gospel." While evangelism is foundational to any missions strategy, missionaries must understand the entirety of the Great Commission and apply it to the local setting. Scripture mandates "making disciples," which encompasses much more than only sharing the gospel. Information gained in the research phase of entry can be helpful to understand worldview, identify specific Bible passages that will speak to that worldview, and learn key language terms to fully communicate the entire gospel message and disciple new believers. Depending on the accessibility of the people group or place, missionaries or mission organizations may have to develop entry strategies to demonstrate the gospel through relief ministries, literacy programs, and healthcare strategies. When using these approaches, one must be careful to avoid the trap of developing a dependency and attracting "rice Christians," those who embrace the foreigner solely for the physical benefits the relationship can bring. Therefore, this leads to the importance of developing appropriate partnerships, a topic that will be addressed in Step Seven.

Discipleship. Missionaries engaging an unreached people or place must always be ready with discipleship strategies to use when the Lord provides fruit from evangelism efforts. The essence of the Great Commission is "making disciples." In order to teach them "to observe everything I have commanded," discipleship is centered on the study of God's Word. This must go beyond the accumulation of knowledge to include discipline and submission to the Word of God that leads to a transformed life. This transformation impacts one's total being, including the heart, mind, affections, will, relationships, and purpose.[2] Christian discipleship is a lifelong endeavor, and transformation can only happen when there is a commitment to the spiritual disciplines of prayer, Bible study, Scripture memory, worship, and Christian service, all in the context of the body of Christ, his church. This leads us to the next component of the Missionary Task.

2. "The Missionary Task," *Foundations,* 84-89.

Healthy Church Formation. The Christian life was not designed to live in isolation, but in relationship to the body of believers. Even in situations where persecution exists and there is need for high security, believers find ways to gather for worship, Bible study, prayer, mutual support, and ministry to the community. Discipleship is most effectively done in the context of the local church.

Churches will look different in different contexts. In some places with space limitations and security restraints, they will take the form of small house churches where only a few people can gather. In other settings they may become large gatherings of believers in rented or even purchased space. Whatever the case, the "Twelve Characteristics of a Healthy Church"[3] can serve as a useful reference to measure the health of the local church. This aspect of the *Missions Continuum* is developed more in our chapter on "Local Ministry: Establishing Healthy Churches" (Step Three), as it is vital to the sending of healthy missionaries.

Leadership Development. Developing leaders is a critical component of the Missionary Task. All churches require local leaders. The apostle Paul provides a great example of this missionary mandate in the way he consistently raised up local leaders to serve as elders or pastors of the churches he was influential in starting. Likewise, from the time a missionary initiates a church-planting strategy, the missionary must have in mind the vision of establishing local leadership. The raising up of local leaders is a fundamental element in establishing healthy local churches.

As God sets apart leaders for his church, pastoral qualifications can be understood in terms of what that leader must BE, must KNOW, and must DO.[4] The quality of a leader's character is the BE characteristic of church leadership. The KNOW characteristic of church leadership is demonstrated in an individual's desire and ability to grow in knowledge, especially in the knowledge of the Word and the desire to gain theological education in the appropriate context for that individual's situation.

---

3. "The Missionary Task," *Foundations*, 7, 90-93.
4. "The Missionary Task," *Foundations*, 94-97.

Finally, the DO characteristic of church leaders should begin with their own practice of spiritual disciplines. Elders and pastors should have the skills necessary to shepherd the local church, which include the ability to teach the Word, with the focus of their pastoral responsibilities "to equip the saints" for ministry (Ephesians 4:12).

Those God has set apart to be leaders in the local church will not be perfect men. However, as missionaries consider individuals for positions of leadership, they should do so by reviewing the biblical qualifications for leadership found in Titus 1:5-9 and 1 Timothy 3:1-7. It is important to recognize that the apostle Paul invested deeply in preparing these servants and recognized that development and training could not be shortchanged. Likewise, in 2 Timothy 2:1-3, Paul implored Timothy to invest in the training and preparation of church leaders. As a cross-cultural missionary trains prospective leaders, some individuals will not prove adequate for the task. Others will demonstrate growth and maturity in the mentoring and training processes to the extent that they can be affirmed by the local church as they demonstrate the BE, KNOW, and DO characteristics.

Exit to Partnership. The goal of the missionary should be to establish healthy churches, and then challenge those fellowships to join in the task of taking the gospel to the unreached with the same goal of planting healthy churches. Ideally, as churches mature, missionaries find they can separate from their initial ministry and focus more on new unreached and unchurched communities. This does not mean abandonment of the missionary's original work; a close relationship of encouragement and training can continue. The apostle Paul maintained relationships with churches he helped establish across the known world. He visited these churches as he had the opportunity, and wrote letters to affirm their growth, challenge them in areas of weakness, and deepen their understanding of the gospel. The essence of Paul's writings is that all churches need to respond to the biblical command to fully embrace the Great Commission. From the very beginning of a new work, the missionary should keep the Great Commission before the people. Then, when the time comes to take the gospel elsewhere, the church is fully on board as the missionary exits to partnership. The foundational premise for the *Eight Steps of the Missions Continuum* is to help churches understand their calling regarding the Great Commission, and make plans and develop partnerships to help them engage in that task.

Abiding in Christ. While each component of the Missionary Task is important, a central element that should undergird all of them is the missionary's focus on abiding in Christ. The spiritual character of the missionary is at the core of the Missionary Task. The most effective missions will be done by those walking closely with the Lord and abiding as his children as noted in Scripture (John 15). Training, expertise, and intelligence will count for nothing if missionaries are not growing disciples themselves. Therefore, abiding in Christ is a critical aspect that permeates the entire process of the Missionary Task.

WHEN THE PROCESS WORKS

IN THE CASE OF THE KRAMER FAMILY, they were likely the right people, and possibly were in the right place had they found a solution to Mike's undiagnosed hearing loss. However, when they deployed it was not the right time. Their lack of understanding of the Missionary Task and what it took to effectively engage the mission field, coupled with their daughter's difficulty in adjustment to overseas life, greatly diminished their effectiveness on the field. In contrast, it is helpful to review a case in which a sending group thoroughly understood the Missionary Task. Because of this, its missionaries were able to sustain their presence and serve as effective gospel witnesses over time.

The island country of Cuba is renowned for its medical schools and the quality of its doctors. Furthermore, in recent decades Cuba has exported thousands of highly skilled medical professionals trained in its system, and many other countries send students to Cuba to receive medical training.

In recent years, Cuban Baptists have been training and sending cross-cultural missionaries from local churches to take the gospel to the most unreached people and places in Latin America. Among these missionaries, several have been doctors who answered God's call to leave Cuba to serve and share the gospel internationally.

One Cuban couple, Raymón and Yolanda García,* moved to Colombia to join an IMB missionary team in a city that bordered an indigenous reservation. Although the missionaries from the US lived nearby, government officials would not allow them access to the reservation. However, when the local Colombian government heard that a Cuban doctor had come to the city, officials approached Dr. García with a proposition. A health official asked Dr. García if he would help train healthcare workers and other medical professionals who lived in twenty-two indigenous villages on the restricted reservation. The Cuban missionary doctor would have full access to enter each one of the villages to train the healthcare workers manning the medical posts on the reservation. The official was aware that this doctor was a missionary because the Garcías reside in Colombia on missionary visas. However, the official wanted to take advantage of this Cuban doctor's skills and his willingness to go into those villages where the country's own Colombian doctors do not want to work.

Because the missionary team the Garcías joined understood the security and political limitations in this situation, they were able to develop strategies to not only gain access but provide credibility by delivering medical care to isolated villages. This consistent access provided the opportunity to share the gospel and follow up in discipleship. In this case, the right people were in the right place at the right time for three important reasons. First, the Cuban missionaries came from a similar culture and already spoke the market language of Spanish. Secondly, the Garcías' medical background allowed them to have access in a place that was previously inaccessible. Finally, it was the right time because government officials recognized their need, and the team in the city provided visas which allowed the missionaries to live in the country. All these factors contributed to the Cuban missionaries' ability to fully engage in the Missionary Task among unreached peoples and facilitated others to join them in the task.

A key to sustaining missionary presence on the mission field is a full understanding of what missionaries actually do in their day-to-day ministry. That means the church, to whom Christ gave the Great Commission, must have a clear understanding of the Missionary Task.

We begin this book with the final step of the *Eight Steps of the Missions Continuum*, because we must be clear about where we want to go and what we want to accomplish when we get there. The *Eight Steps* process is a way to build a bridge all the way from the local church to the mission field. Once the vision of the destination is clear, we can step back to consider each step along the way. The next chapter of this book will discuss the importance of the local pastor to the mission of motivating the local church toward a Great Commission vision.

2

STEP ONE

The Local Pastor

Expanding the Vision of the Local Church

S OFIA* IS A MISSIONS MOBILIZER in her local church. Years ago, she learned about missions when a cross-cultural missionary working in her Latin American city discipled her. And as Sofia delved into Scripture, Acts 1:8 deeply impressed her: ". . . and you will be my witnesses in Jerusalem, in all Judea and Samaria, and to the ends of the earth." Sofia's love for Jesus and her desire to see multitudes of people from every nation worshipping Christ became her life's focus.

Yet, at that time, the pastor of her church was mainly interested in planting satellite churches around their city. Pastor Alejandro* had a vision for reaching his city for Christ, but not beyond, and certainly not for reaching the nations. As the only minister in the church, he spent most of his time pastoring his flock and leading local ministries that might result in new satellite church plants. Pastor Alejandro did not have the time and energy to focus on much more. While Sofia supported her pastor's vision, involving herself in community outreach and evangelism, she also felt the church was not fully obeying the Great Commission, and certainly was not focusing on peoples beyond their city who did not have a gospel witness.

When Sofia told Pastor Alejandro that she felt God's call to take the gospel to the lost people of South Asia, he was resistant. Sofia had pursued theological education and had even connected with a sending agency. But though Pastor Alejandro eventually agreed that she could go to South Asia, he told her that the church would not support her financially, as her desire to serve in another country didn't fit the church's ministry plan. She ultimately raised support from friends, family, and other churches, and moved to South Asia where she joined a missionary team already in place.

When she wrote home to her church members to share with them what God was doing among the Hindus in South Asia, some did not understand why she was there when so many people in their own city had not heard the gospel. Eventually, Sofia's financial support dwindled, and her team sent her home to raise more support so she could return. Back in Latin America, she shared testimonies of how God had used her to reach many men, women, and families with the gospel. But even then, her church and pastor continued to be unsupportive, and she could not raise the funds she needed to return. What had been a fruitful ministry in South Asia seemed over. One missionary teammate, however, suggested that perhaps God had different plans for her; perhaps her return to her home country was to mobilize the church to send many more missionaries to be a light among the lost in South Asia.

When she shared this with her friend Daniela,* who also had a passion for international missions, they decided to begin praying for all the pastors and churches in their city to become Great Commission churches. They prayed that when local pastors read their Bibles, they would see the Great Commission throughout Scripture and begin to mobilize their churches to reach the unreached, both in their city and abroad.

Sofia joined Daniela's home church, led by Pastor Mateo.* Though the church's mission statement was "to form generations of believers who impact the city and the world with the powerful Word of the gospel of Jesus Christ," Pastor Mateo was much like other pastors in the area; most were busy and overburdened with local ministries rather than focusing on sending out missionaries to the nations. Furthermore, when Sofia and Daniela asked Pastor Mateo if they could organize a missions committee in their church to promote reaching the nations, he refused and only allowed them to hold an event to talk about missions. Instead of criticizing church leadership, the two women continued to support their pastor's vision and church ministries as they prayed for God to open Pastor Mateo's heart for the nations.

Eventually, Daniela and Sofia invited Pastor Mateo to attend an international missions conference with them, and he accepted. They paid for him to go and prayed the Lord would open his eyes to see God's heart for the nations. God finally answered their prayer: At the conference, the Lord moved Pastor Mateo's heart with compassion for the billions of unreached people throughout the world. Since that time, Pastor Mateo has led his church in an Acts 1:8 missions strategy that includes local, national, and international ministry.

THE PASTOR IS THE GATEWAY TO THE CHURCH

SOFIA'S STORY IS NOT UNCOMMON. If the pastor does not have a Great Commission vision to "make disciples of all nations," then his church will not have it either. As we have consulted with partners in many countries, believers have approached us who want to leave their churches because their pastors are not supportive of their desire and call to serve in international missions. Too often pastors and church leaders mainly focus on growing their flock, and perhaps even their influence in their community, rather than on growing God's kingdom. Sofia and Daniela trusted the Lord to transform their pastor and church through his Word and through the work of the Holy Spirit. They prayed fervently for Pastor Mateo and continued to use their gifts in local church ministries until the pastor was ready to lead his church to be fully missional.

But this is not everyone's story. God has entrusted pastors with the health and growth of their flocks. Peter, in his first epistle, exhorts leaders of the churches to "Shepherd God's flock among you, not overseeing out of compulsion but willingly, as God would have you; not out of greed for money but eagerly; not lording it over those entrusted to you, but being examples to the flock" (1 Peter 5:2-3). It is an enormous responsibility to teach sound doctrine and move a congregation toward spiritual maturity. All pastors sincerely want to do God's will and lead their people to be transformed into the image of Christ, and to be a light in their communities.

Also, all pastors, like Pastor Alejandro and Pastor Mateo, are busy and carry heavy burdens. Both in the United States as well as all over the world, many churches are led by only one pastor, who is the sole staff member of the church. Often these pastors are bivocational as well. They are expected to preach interesting and engaging sermons every week. They visit the sick and the lonely. They console families at funerals and celebrate with families by officiating at weddings. They help settle marital disputes and counsel parents and teenagers who are at odds. Even the best and most godly of pastors have weighty responsibilities and need the support and encouragement of the members of their congregations. And in everything, they are to be examples to their members. Alone, this is a heavy burden to bear.

REASONS FOR RELUCTANCE

WITH THE MANY CARES that make it difficult for pastors to think about embracing the Great Commission vision, what are some of their major concerns when it comes to sending out their own members as international missionaries? When we ask pastors, missionaries, and church members this question at consultations, they answer with common themes. Here are the top ten reasons we've heard why pastors do not send out cross-cultural missionaries:

- If I send missionaries, I will lose my best people.
- If I send missionaries, it will cost us money, and the church barely gives enough to support me [the pastor] and the ministries of the church.
- I want to reach our local community and bring more people into our church.
- I must protect my leadership position. I can't let others dictate the direction of my church.
- I don't know how to train cross-cultural missionaries because my church is monocultural.
- I am the only minister here. I don't have the time and energy to start international ministries.
- My people aren't even involved in local ministry.
- Other pastors in the area are not doing international missions either.
- What if I send missionaries and they fail?
- I don't trust mission-sending organizations.

How can church members help pastors to address these issues? Should a church member who feels called to go to the nations leave his local church if the pastor does not have an international ministry strategy? How might Sofia have better supported her first pastor and helped him to have a vision for the nations before she went to South Asia so that her ministry there would have been an extension of the ministry of her church? How can church members better support and encourage pastors?

THE MISSIONAL BASIS OF THE BIBLE

THE MOST EFFECTIVE WAY for a church to become a missional church is for the pastor to preach the Bible and cast vision for the church to know and proclaim God's heart for the nations. The Bible is God's revelation of his plan and character to us. A thread of God's heart for the nations runs through both the Old and New Testaments. The first account of God's redemptive plan for all nations is foreshadowed in Genesis 3:15, when after the fall, God curses the serpent that Satan embodied, and tells it, "I will put hostility between you and the woman, and between your offspring and her offspring. He will strike your head, and you will strike his heel." God's plan from the beginning was to rescue man from the evil schemes of Satan by a descendant of Eve.

Next, in Genesis 12:1-3 we clearly see God's plan to draw all nations to himself in his call to Abram. The Lord said to Abram:

> *Go from your land,*
> *your relatives,*
> *and your father's house*
> *to the land that I will show you.*
> *I will make you into a great nation,*
> *I will bless you,*
> *I will make your name great,*
> *and you will be a blessing.*
> *I will bless those who bless you,*
> *I will curse anyone who treats you with contempt,*
> *and all the peoples on earth*
> *will be blessed through you.*

We see the same promise to Abram, now called Abraham, again in Genesis 22 when God tests Abraham. In verse 18, God says, "And all the nations of the earth will be blessed by your offspring because you have obeyed my command."

The Psalms are replete with proclamations of God's heart for the nations. Psalm 96:1-3 proclaims:

> *Sing a new song to the Lord;*
> *let the whole earth sing to the Lord.*
> *Sing to the Lord, bless his name;*
> *proclaim his salvation from day to day.*
> *Declare his glory among the nations,*
> *his wondrous works among all peoples.*

The prophets also were inspired to tell the nations to prepare for God's deliverance. For example, Isaiah 49:5-6 says:

And now, says the Lord,
who formed me from the womb to be his servant,
to bring Jacob back to him
so that Israel might be gathered to him;
for I am honored in the sight of the Lord,
and my God is my strength—
he says,
"It is not enough for you to be my servant
raising up the tribes of Jacob
and restoring the protected ones of Israel.
I will also make you a light for the nations,
to be my salvation to the ends of the earth."

Of course, in the New Testament, the church received the mandate of the Great Commission directly from our Lord Jesus Christ. All four gospels and the book of Acts record Jesus commanding his followers to make disciples of all nations by the power of the Holy Spirit. (See Matthew 28:18-20, Mark 16:14-16, Luke 24:46-49, John 20:21-23, and Acts 1:8.)

In Acts 2, we see that promise fulfilled when the Holy Spirit descends upon Jews from "every nation under heaven" hearing the magnificent acts of God in their own languages. In Acts 8, when persecution scatters the believers, they take the gospel to Samaria. There Philip shares the gospel with the Ethiopian eunuch, who becomes the first baptized Gentile.

In Acts 10, God uses a vision to show Peter that ". . .God doesn't show favoritism, but in every nation the person who fears him and does what is right is acceptable to him. He sent the message to the Israelites, proclaiming the good news of peace through Jesus Christ—he is Lord of all" (Acts 10:34-36).

Then, in Acts 13:1-3, we see the church at Antioch—a multiethnic church—worshipping together. The Holy Spirit directs the church to set apart Saul and Barnabas to be sent out as missionaries.

And the story goes on and on until "This good news of the kingdom will be proclaimed in all the world as a testimony to all nations, and then the end will come" (Matthew 24:14). As believers, therefore, we have a biblical mandate to not only make disciples of all nations, but to make disciples who make disciples. As Paul instructed Timothy, "What you have heard from me in the presence of many witnesses, commit to faithful men who will be able to teach others also" (2 Timothy 2:2).

This is not an exhaustive Bible study of the missional basis of God's Word here. There are many books and articles already written that will help you to follow the missional plan of God from Genesis to Revelation. The point is that the Bible reveals that it was God's plan from before the creation of the world to make a way to bring sinful mankind into a relationship with him—a holy God. He was not only saving the nation of Israel for himself, but he was making a way for everyone who believes in him, including the Gentiles, to have eternal life (John 3:16).

The vision that John reveals of what heaven looks like in Revelation 7:9 includes people from every nation: "After this I looked, and there was a vast multitude from every nation, tribe, people, and language, which no one could number, standing before the throne and before the Lamb." Therefore, we know that it is essential for the church and for every believer to be involved in making disciples of all nations.

The pastor has the responsibility to teach the Word to his congregation. If he preaches the whole Bible story, God's mission will come through in every sermon, in every Bible study, in every activity of the church. As the pastor faithfully teaches the whole Word of God to his congregation, casting vision for God's heart for the nations, then his members will be mobilized for ministry and missions, and his church will grow. God will provide the resources to do his will.

In Ephesians 4:11-13, Paul explains this principle to the Ephesian church: "And he himself gave some to be apostles, some prophets, some evangelists, some pastors and teachers, to equip the saints for the work of ministry, to build up the body of Christ, until we all reach unity in the faith and in the knowledge of God's Son, growing into maturity with a stature measured by Christ's fullness." As he equips the saints to use their spiritual gifts for the ministries of the church, God will raise up missionaries who go, and he will raise up leaders to take their places in the local church. He will also equip the church to send those he has called. As the pastor leads the church to fully embrace the Great Commission, the church will be mobilized to join the pastor in ministering locally as well. The Great Commission begins with ministry in the local community, and then spreads beyond. Then, the pastor is not carrying the whole ministry load himself, but each church member can come alongside the pastor in fulfilling the Great Commission. We cannot pursue God's mission without depending on his provision and his faithfulness.

Will the pastor lose some of his most active and faithful disciples to missions and other ministries? Absolutely. That is the goal of 2 Timothy 2:1-3. There is a price for being involved in God's mission. There is a sacrifice we make. But in making those sacrifices out of obedience to the Great Commission, God will bless and multiply for the sake of his kingdom.

THE RESULTS OF OBEDIENCE

WHEN PASTOR MATEO RETURNED to his church from the international missions conference he attended with Sofia and Daniela, God had changed his heart. He wanted his whole church to be involved in proclaiming the gospel to the unreached of the world, beginning in his community, then spreading to the ends of the earth.

Now, Pastor Mateo says, "If the pastor of a church is mobilized to take the gospel to the nations, he will mobilize the whole church." Working from an Acts 1:8 missions strategy, he has teams who plan for missions locally, regionally, and globally. His members, like Sofia, also work to mobilize other pastors and churches in their city to work together to reach the nations with the gospel. This Great Commission focus has actually brought growth to his church, and the congregation is now sending out missionaries to the nations, and fully supporting them financially and with prayer. Pastor Mateo has also mobilized other pastors in his denomination to work together to send and sustain even more missionaries.

MOVING FORWARD

ONCE THE PASTOR HAS A HEART to not only grow his church, but to take the gospel to the nations, he can mobilize his whole church to have the same heart. He can explain in simple ways how the whole church can be involved in God's mission. Essentially, he is helping his church embrace God's heart for the nations.

As we have led the *Eight Steps of the Missions Continuum* consultations, pastors and churches in similar situations have been able to develop action plans to move their missions vision forward. In the next step, we will look at how a pastor can mobilize his whole church, from the youngest to the oldest members, to be involved in the ministry of the church, thus embracing their role in the Great Commission, and in the meantime, growing the local church and God's kingdom.

_3_

Church Mobilization

A S WE SAW IN STEP ONE, the pastor of the local church is key in mobilizing his church for ministry. Every pastor wants God's best for his church and wants to see his congregation growing in spiritual depth, ministry to the community, and in numbers. But how can a pastor cast the vision of God's heart for the nations to his whole church so that every member can be equipped and using his or her spiritual gifts in ministering to the body and the community?

Here is an example of how the pastors and elders of one US church have equipped and mobilized all members for ministry, from the youngest to the oldest.

GRACE COMMUNITY BAPTIST CHURCH: "FROM K TO KITTY"

GRACE COMMUNITY BAPTIST CHURCH is a fellowship of about 150 families in Richmond, Virginia. In its thirty-six-year history, this congregation has sent and sustained dozens of long-term missionaries to the nations through various partner organizations. Missions is not a just part of what the members do; it is their purpose. The church has active local and international missions teams who plan ministries and activities year-round to keep the Great Commission at the forefront of everything they do.

Each year during the Christmas season, pastors and elders challenge each person in their body of believers to be involved in all aspects of missions. In addition to contributing to the annual missions offering, each family or individual is challenged to commit to the following activities throughout the coming year:

1. Pray for the salvation of unreached people groups around the world and for each missionary that has been sent from Grace Community, whether serving domestically or overseas. Members are also asked to pray for their neighbors. Finally, the church challenges members to ask the Lord how he would have them be involved in the mission of the church.
2. Give generously and sacrificially to all missions efforts of the church.
3. Go on a mission trip, whether it's serving at the local crisis pregnancy center, doing short-term work in another state, or spending the summer working alongside other Grace Community missionaries overseas.

The pastors challenge every person who is able to be involved, from the youngest to elderly members of the church. Even the kindergarteners are taught that they can pray, give from their allowances, and minister to their friends, family, and neighbors. The oldest member of the congregation is a woman called Mrs. Kitty. Because of her advanced years, Mrs. Kitty cannot travel overseas, but she is known as the fiercest prayer warrior in the church, hosting a time of prayer in her home each Friday morning at 6:00. She also eats breakfast at a local restaurant several mornings each week so that she can meet new people, share the gospel with them, and pray for them.

So, at Grace Community Baptist Church, the slogan is that everyone, "from K [kindergarteners] to Kitty," must be involved in missions: in praying, giving, and going, all year long. This is an example of the entire church effectively mobilized for missions. All members can be involved in sending others, and God will call a few to be "goers." Those who are "senders," supporting through prayer and giving, should be embedded in the fabric of the church—right down through every age group—as in the example from Grace Community. Missions education is not an add-on to the church training program; it should be at the very core, because taking the gospel to the nations is the responsibility of the church.

EQUIPPING THE CHURCH

A KEY RESPONSIBILITY OF THE PASTOR is to equip his congregation so all believers can use their spiritual gifts in ministering to the church and to the lost, both in the local community and abroad. Paul tells the Ephesian church that Christ "gave some to be apostles, some prophets, some evangelists, some pastors and teachers, to equip the saints for the work of ministry, to build up the body of Christ" (Ephesians 4:11-12). When a pastor casts the missions vision, however, it is common for members of his congregation to raise questions—questions not every pastor may feel comfortable answering. For example, a member may approach the pastor asking: "How can we afford to divert resources to a mission field somewhere else when there are so many lost people in our area?" At that point, the pastor needs to be prepared with Scripture-based answers and to help that member understand the role of the church in the Great Commission.

We have designed the *Eight Steps* consultation to equip pastors to be able to answer these questions, relying on the Word of God. Building a solid foundation is critical for the missions vision to catch on within the local church. Luke 6:46-49 emphasized the importance of a house built on a firm foundation. When the flood comes, the house built on the rock stands firm. The house with no solid foundation is washed away in the midst of the flood. The passage challenges the reader to be a doer, acting on the commands of Scripture. When we respond in this way, our house will stand. Therefore, a missions vision built on the Word of God will stand the test of time and provide a firm foundation whereby a missions plan and strategy (see Step Five) can be implemented with consistency and sustainability.

There are six relevant questions a pastor should address when casting a missions vision within his church. A pastor may choose to preach a sermon series, write articles, or develop small group Bible studies to answer what we call "The Six Critical Questions" about missions involvement for the local church. These questions are:

1. What is missions?
2. Why should we do missions?
3. When should we do missions?
4. Where should we do missions?
5. Who should do missions?
6. How should we do missions?

What is missions? It is interesting to hear various definitions for "missions" involvement from church members. They often mention many worthwhile activities, with "sharing the gospel" as the most common answer. In reality, missions is a huge umbrella that can encompass disaster relief, human needs and development, medical, agricultural, and educational ministries. All of these activities, however, done without gospel proclamation, do not describe the biblical concept of missions. In defining missions, we must also consider the distinction between ongoing evangelism and discipleship within the local church, and the mandate from Scripture to "make disciples of all nations," the Great Commission given to the church. Matthew 24:14 indicates that the gospel must be preached to all peoples before the Lord returns. We do not determine when the Lord chooses to return, but we should recognize that the biblical mandate for the church is to proclaim the gospel to the ends of the earth to all who need to hear. Missions is the concept that encompasses all of this. At the core of missions is the gospel, and sharing that gospel with all peoples.

Missions is also coupled with the promises of God, such as his promise to be with us always (Matthew 28). It ultimately culminates with the vision from Revelation 7:9 which indicates that the mission will be successful, as the Lord promises that every nation, people, language and tribe will have representatives worshipping the Lord in heaven.

Why should we do missions? This is especially important to address for members asking why a church should focus on the nations, when there are so many lost individuals in a local community, town, city or region. The answer, again, comes from Scripture. The world is lost and facing judgment (Hebrews 9:27). God loves the world, sent Jesus to save mankind (John 3:16-17), and outside of Jesus, there is no salvation (Acts 4:12, John 14:6). Acts 1:8 casts the vision beyond the local church to the ends of the earth, not forgetting Judea and Samaria. The passage does not define a timeline or church maturity level necessary to fully embrace the mission, nor is the task linear. Romans 10:13-15 indicates that the lost will not hear without a preacher, or proclaimer. Therefore, the church must intentionally seek the Lord's leading in reaching out to their Jerusalem, Judea, Samaria, and also the ends of the earth (Matthew 28:16-20). The mission of the church encompasses the entire world, and how to specifically embrace that commission should be a matter of prayer and church discussion. Step Five, "Planning for Cross-Cultural Missions," provides some excellent ways for a church to start with a systematic plan. Seeking the Lord in prayer as a body of believers is the key first step.

When should we do missions? Response to this question must be a balance between adequate preparation and timing, along with sensitivity to the urgency for the task. With thousands of people dying each day without the Lord, time is critical for those whose lives may end without a chance to respond to the gospel. The Acts 13 passage, in which the Holy Spirit calls Paul and Barnabas, indicates the Lord will show a church the right time to send out missionaries with prompting by the Spirit. In John 4, Jesus challenges his disciples when he interacts with the Samaritan woman at the well. Not only does he challenge their prejudice against women and the Samaritans, but he also indicates that the fields are "ready for harvest" (John 4:35). We recognize in Luke 19:10 that the whole purpose of Jesus' coming is to "seek and to save the lost." We, therefore, should also be about this task. With this emphasis from Scripture, even in the early stages of a new church plant, the Great Commission should be kept in view and the church should plan intentionally, seeking the leading of the Lord to define its role in his mission, the Great Commission.

Where should we do missions? The "where" question of missions must be answered in terms of "Who needs the gospel?" We cannot choose only those places that integrate easily with our own culture and understanding. Some must be willing to take the gospel to peoples and places very foreign to them, and among peoples whose lives are vastly different, with perhaps some aspects of their culture even seeming offensive. So, the question of where to commit to missions activity can begin with an assessment of our own perceptions of people different from ourselves.

Often US churches are monocultural in their membership. If so, members may not have the opportunity to associate with and know people of different ethnicities, languages, and countries of origin. Acts 10 is an excellent passage for both the church and missionary candidates to study to assess any prejudices they might have toward others. In Acts 10, the vision and voice of the Lord challenged Peter to consider his prejudices against Gentiles, and Romans specifically, especially the occupying Roman army. With this vision, God demonstrated to Peter that Jewish Christians should share the gospel with Gentiles—a people Peter considered unclean. He had to overcome that difference for the sake of the gospel. As a result, Cornelius and his household believed and were baptized. Therefore, we must all explore our personal prejudices. However, that is only a part of helping the church decide where to be involved.

Sometimes we must consider opportunity. Has God given a specific opportunity for ministry via access or relationships within the church that bring the unreached to mind? There are times when a church may have a particular refugee community in its vicinity and seeks to engage them locally as well as back in their home country. Sometimes the church embraces the specific calling of its members by joining them in partnership to reach a particular unreached people or place. In Step Five, we will challenge the church to develop a plan to begin with praying together for the nations and seeking the Lord's leading as to where the church should be involved.

Who should do missions? The question is not who should be a gospel witness, as that task belongs to all believers, as "he has committed the message of reconciliation to us" (2 Corinthians 5:17-19). Rather, the question is: who is God calling to cross barriers—geographical, cultural, religious, and linguistic—to take the gospel message to unreached peoples and places? Scripture should cast the vision. This may be done through the preaching ministry, but may also occur through discipleship classes and mentorships, children's studies, and opportunities for cross-cultural mission experiences. The Holy Spirit can use individuals' exposure to God's Word and opportunities to experience the mission field firsthand to call believers to missionary service. It is important for the church to provide an atmosphere where this can transpire. The Bible studies presented in Step Four, "Raising up Missionaries," can be helpful in walking through this process with missionary candidates. The missionary is called by God and set apart by the church to cross various boundaries to take the gospel to the unreached. All believers are called to be "witnesses," but only some are called to be missionaries.

How should we do missions? When this question is being asked it is probably a time to celebrate, as the other questions have been answered and members are at the point of wanting to know what they can do. The entire *Eight Steps* process helps answer this question: how do we implement the Missionary Task among unreached peoples and places? The church has a role, and each individual has a role. The more this is done in community—praying, studying Scripture, and seeking the Lord together—the more unified the church will be in its missions vision. This does not mean that everyone does the same thing, but that they are together with one mind and one heart, united toward a common purpose as described in Philippians 2:1-3. Members should recognize that all have a Great Commission calling. Some are to "send," and some are to "go." We can all get involved in the sending part immediately, and in that process, God will call out some to explore the calling to go as missionaries, taking the gospel to unreached peoples and places.

The pastor is key in casting the missions vision, but it is critical for every member to embrace the vision and accept their part. The "K to Kitty" approach from Grace Community Baptist Church is an excellent model. The more thoroughly the vision is adopted by the church, the more prayer, giving, and personal involvement there will be in accomplishing that vision. Hebrews 11:6 states that "without faith it is impossible to please God." That is the case in adopting a missions vision. As we pray and follow that prayer with action, the Lord will affirm and direct our steps to fully embrace what he has for the church, and especially the whole church's role in the Great Commission.

4

Local Ministry

Establishing Healthy Churches

S OMETIMES we mistake outward appearance for health. This can happen easily even with those we know well. What we see on the outside does not always reflect the health on the inside. Consider this personal account by one of the authors:

I felt I was getting along just fine physically. Yet, an annual physical exam revealed something very different. A hunch by an examining physician led to more blood tests, an MRI, and finally a biopsy that revealed the disease we all fear: cancer. I was shocked. I felt fine, had no symptoms, and could not understand how a potentially cat-astrophic disease could be lurking in my body. But the cancer diag-nosis was definitive, and I needed a specific treatment or the disease was likely to spread to other parts of my body. Doctors established an extensive treatment plan which I completed over a period of months. The treatment was invasive and at times painful. Yet now, doctors say I am healthy and cancer-free. Had it not been for the diagnosis and my willingness to follow the treatment, the cancer could easily have spread to other parts of my body, wreaking havoc on my system and causing serious illness or death if left unchecked.

One might ask, what does this have to do with local ministry and healthy churches? Just as with our personal health, unless there is careful examination, one may never diagnose the actual health of a church. And when it comes to sending missionaries, a spiritually healthy church will be more likely to send spiritually healthy missionaries. Similarly, spiri-tually unhealthy churches are more likely to send spiritually unhealthy missionaries. A missionary who is not spiritually healthy is not prepared for the rigors of cross-cultural missions, may have difficulty adjusting to the challenges, and will rarely sustain presence on the field.

The Lighthouse Church* in Asia had experienced steady growth since its establishment in the mid-1990s. The church had many musically tal-ented youth and young adults who made the worship time professional, joyous, and uplifting. Numerous language groups attended, so the church provided translation in the preaching services. Recognizing the need for deeper, personal discipleship, the church also established discipleship groups throughout the city of about 1 million people. These well-attended groups met in homes, restaurants, and coffee shops. Once a month on Sunday afternoons, the senior pastor trained the small group leaders, giv-ing them Bible study materials for four weeks at a time. The small groups had active prayer ministries and they devoted much of their small group session time to prayer and ministering to the needs of the group members.

When we were invited as a consultancy team to teach these group lead-ers on the principles of servant leadership, small group dynamics, and transformative discipleship, about fifty gathered, representing the small groups that met across the entire city. We used an analysis tool adapted from the Church Circles mapping process in *Four Fields of Kingdom Growth*[5] to gather from these leaders information with which to assess the health status of the church. The results were surprising.

The assessment asks participants to review Acts 2 along with other Scripture passages that describe the early church, identifying characteristics as it was being established. Participants are then asked to look for the presence of those characteristics within their own church. Additionally, the group looked at the "Twelve Characteristics of a Healthy Church"[6] and the small group leaders completed individual assessments. The survey of these fifty leaders revealed several characteristics in their church that they deemed strong, such as worship, prayer, giving, and fellowship. However, biblical preaching and discipleship received lower marks and were areas cited as needing the most improvement. These results were a surprise to the pastor and to us as the consultancy team. We had anticipated that discipleship and preaching would be among the strengths of this church.

While the assessment identified the problem, it did not clarify the reason for the problem. The pastor invested considerable time in preparing sermons, referring to commentaries, and praying for the right topics to help the church. He also spent ample time preparing the lessons for the small group leaders, giving them the content needed to adequately lead their respective groups. We held a follow-up discussion with the small group leaders to ask why these two areas were noted as problems. They recognized that the pastor prepared biblical sermons, and there was no concern with the content. But our discussion revealed that often the sermons were too academic for church members, especially those who were new believers.

---

5. Nathan and Kari Shank, *Four Fields of Kingdom Growth: Starting and Releasing Healthy Churches* (2007, rev. 2014), https://static1.squarespace.com/static/588ada483a0411a-f1ab3e7ca/t/58a40ef11b631bcbd49c88c0/1487146760589/4-Fields-Nathan-Shank-2014.pdf.

6. "Twelve Characteristics of a Healthy Church," in *Foundations* (Richmond, VA: IMB, 2018), 7, 61-64.

Members had a difficult time understanding the concepts and could not make connections to their daily lives. Many were first-generation believers, still carrying some of the baggage of their lives before Christ. Many had been versed in traditional Asian religions from birth and were dealing with persecution within their own families. These members possessed few handles on how to deal with these family issues. The small group leaders expressed a sincere need to have sermons that dealt with the conflicting worldviews: the Christian worldview and the various Asian worldviews from which they came. For example, one leader mentioned the need for understanding how the Bible addresses the honor-shame culture that so permeates their local society. Another issue was how they could they better understand the sacrifice of Jesus on the cross as they contrast his sacrifice with the temple sacrificial system that surrounds local beliefs. They needed direct application of biblical teaching to their everyday lives so they could have answers to these deep, troubling questions.

As a result, the pastor changed his approach. He presented a sermon series dealing with some of these cultural issues, taking the opportunity to teach the biblical culture contrasted with the false teachings of the day. The small groups then became safe places where people could ask questions about the sermon and seek clarification from their small group leaders. Six months later, results from a follow-up assessment were much different. What was initially considered a weakness of the church had become a strength. The pastor had adjusted his Bible preaching and teaching to make a direct impact on peoples' lives rather than delivering the more academic theological discourse members had experienced in the past.

TWELVE CHARACTERISTICS OF A HEALTHY CHURCH

WE ARE REMINDED that appearance does not always reflect reality, or in the case of the local church, does not reflect church health based on biblical standards. Too often we use megachurches or those with innovative worship services as models of church health for others to replicate. When we review the biblical model of church, we recognize that size and worship style are not the standards for assessment.

In IMB missions, the definition of church from the "Baptist Faith and Message" serves as our standard:

A New Testament church of the Lord Jesus Christ is an autonomous local congregation of baptized believers, associated by covenant in the faith and fellowship of the gospel; observing the two ordinances of Christ, governed by His laws, exercising the gifts, rights, and privileges invested in them by His word, and seeking to extend the gospel to the ends of the earth. Each congregation operates under the lordship of Christ through democratic processes. In such a congregation each member is responsible and accountable to Christ as Lord. Its scriptural officers are pastors and deacons. While both men and women are gifted for service in the church, the office of pastor is limited to men as qualified by Scripture.

The New Testament speaks also of the church as the Body of Christ which includes all of the redeemed of all the ages, believers from every tribe, and tongue, and people, and nation.[7]

The measure of a healthy church is more of a qualitative measurement of the twelve characteristics as outlined in *Foundations*.[8] Those twelve characteristics are:

1. *Biblical Evangelism* — Acts 2:38
2. *Biblical Discipleship* — Acts 2:42, Matthew 28:19-20
3. *Biblical Preaching and Teaching* — Acts 2:42
4. *Biblical Leadership* — Acts 2:42, 1 Timothy 3:1-7, Titus 1:5-9
5. *Biblical Membership* — Acts 2:46, 1 Corinthians 12
6. *Biblical Worship* — Acts 2:47
7. *Biblical Fellowship* — Acts 2:46
8. *Biblical Prayer* — Acts 2:42

---

7. Southern Baptist Convention, "Baptist Faith and Message, 2000," Statement of Faith, https://bfm.sbc.net/bfm2000/#vi-the-church (accessed January 21, 2022).

8. "Twelve Characteristics of a Healthy Church," *Foundations*, 61-64.

9. *Biblical Accountability and Discipline* — Acts 2:40, Matthew 18:15-17
10. *Biblical Giving* — Acts 2:45
11. *Biblical Ordinances of Baptism and the Lord's Supper* — Acts 2:38, 41; Matthew 26:26-29
12. *Biblical Mission* — Matthew 28:16-20, Matthew 24:14

In our consultancies, we often refer to this step as "local ministry" as well as "healthy church." The goal is to focus our attention on the local church. The foundation of God's kingdom on earth is his church. Scripture tells us that ". . .the gates of Hades will not overpower it" (Matthew 16:18). When it comes to fully embracing the challenge of the Great Commission, making disciples of all nations, God's church must be as healthy as possible to be ready for such a formidable task.

As we study the concept of local ministry, we recognize that it encompasses all aspects of the local church, essentially touching on each of the twelve characteristics. Biblical leadership is necessary to lead the church and "to equip the saints for the work of ministry, to build up the body of Christ," as commanded in Ephesians 4:11-12. Biblical preaching and discipleship are necessary to help believers mature, guiding them toward understanding their spiritual gifts and how to use those gifts in service through the local church. Accountability, which goes along with biblical membership and discipline, helps keep the church pure and ensures that false teaching and sinful behaviors do not creep in to weaken the body. The ordinances of baptism and the Lord's Supper provide an outward testimony of the inward change which results with our salvation and the work of the Holy Spirit in our lives. Biblical worship, prayer, and fellowship strengthen the body of Christ and prepare us to face a lost world and support each other as we walk through life. Biblical giving is returning a portion to the Lord of what he has provided for each of us. Evangelism is a core function of the church as members engage in the ministry of reconciliation (2 Corinthians 5:17-19). Finally, biblical mission is embracing our role in the Great Commission. The Great Commission is defined and clarified in many passages, but all are clear that the church has responsibilities in the local context as well as in helping to take the gospel to the ends of the earth, to those who have never heard.

BEGINNING IN OUR JERUSALEM

THE LOCAL CHURCH can see its health and readiness for missions in the status of its local ministry. Members of the church should be using their spiritual gifts in service to the church. If the pastor is the only ministry-giver, his church members do not have the opportunity to minister to one another and the surrounding community. Basic discipleship for all ages is at the core of this task, which includes the study and application of Scripture. The pastor should understand the characteristics of a healthy church, then move his church toward becoming healthier. Assessing a church's strengths and weaknesses is an important early step in helping the church embrace God's mission for the nations.

While conducting an *Eight Steps* consultancy in an Asian capital city, we learned of a church's desire to share the gospel with unreached peoples in a remote section of the country. A survey trip had confirmed that most in that area identified as Muslims, though underneath the veneer of Islam, their daily practices revealed beliefs influenced by animism. The church had begun praying for this people and investigating how it could partner with others to send workers to share the gospel there. They recognized that the language and culture were very different from their own, and that it would require a great effort by the church and the missionaries selected to carry out this task.

As we worked through each of the *Eight Steps* with these leaders, the discussion of what constitutes a healthy church hit a nerve among several in the group, causing them to see the ministry of their church in a very different way. They agreed that the Muslim peoples God had placed on their heart in a distant land needed a missionary to enter their world and learn language and culture to be able to share the gospel message. But as they studied the challenges of ministry and crossing into that culture, they also recognized their shortcomings in understanding how to do Muslim ministry. They felt a need to give potential missionaries from their church some first-hand experience in working with Muslims locally before sending them to a remote part of the country. Additionally, they realized missions outreach in their community would build awareness among members in their church, encouraging the whole congregation to be part of this ministry endeavor as well.

As our discussion progressed into "Selecting and Training Cross-Cultural Missionaries" (Step Six), the pastor of the group suddenly stood up and stated that he now realized what the Lord had been saying to him. He had recently discovered a Muslim reading room in their community not far from the building where their church met. When he asked how many were aware of this reading room, the response was that no one knew it even existed. He then asked how many in the group had Muslim friends or acquaintances. The response was unanimous—not one had a Muslim friend. With the pastor realizing there were many Muslims in their own neighborhood, he proposed that their church should evaluate ways to reach out to them.

This did not diminish their sense of call to send missionaries to the more isolated part of the country, but it demonstrated that right there in their "own backyard" was a training ground for future missionaries and for the local church to learn about Muslim ministry as members reached out to these neighbors. The resulting effort strengthened the local church by ministering to the lost in its community and showing God's love in tangible ways. It also presented an opportunity for those feeling called to work among Muslims in the remote location to practice and test that calling by reaching out to the Muslims living next door.

There are times when the best strategy to participate in the Great Commission is to strengthen the local church. This is not easy. Church leaders and members must be willing to be transparent, take a careful look at the biblical models for church, and prayerfully consider areas of church life that the Lord would have them strengthen. There are also times when there are no visible signs of poor church health. However, once church leaders identify weaknesses, they can work with their members to develop action plans to make the necessary changes. Ultimately, healthy churches are more likely to equip and send healthy and effective missionaries, while unhealthy churches are more likely to send missionaries who have difficulty adjusting to the challenges of the mission field and therefore contribute to the high attrition rates of sending churches and agencies.

For any of the *Eight Steps* to have significant impact, the emphasis on this Step Three and the local church, should receive careful attention. Weaknesses in church health can severely hamper a church's development in other steps. However, a strong effort towards local ministry and church health can launch a congregation into a process of building the bridge from the church to the mission field and helping a church fully embrace its role in the Great Commission.

5

STEP FOUR

Raising Up Missionaries

T HE FIRST MISSIONS CONFERENCE in this small rural network of churches in Southeast Asia drew about forty attendees from various ethnic groups—all who made their living by farming the rugged mountain slopes of this region. The gospel had come to this area more than a decade before and the number of believers had continued to grow. The missionaries who brought the gospel had focused on discipleship and leadership training, and there was exceptional fruit from those endeavors. Though persecution had made the early years difficult, it had waned as authorities recognized how much Christians added to the economic and social well-being of the area. While only limited government resources were available to these communities, a generation before this time the government had introduced education up to the fourth-grade level. Many believers spoke their village dialect, but also now had access to a translation of God's Word in the market language, the language of education.

We met in a converted farmhouse that was hardly conducive to a missions conference. Nevertheless, participants were excited and there was a sense that the Great Commission was given to all of God's people—even humble farmers. As they listened to the vision for missions, participants began to identify the many different peoples living right there in their own community. Most admitted they had avoided getting to know these individuals because they spoke different languages, wore different clothes, and even ate different foods. Once participants realized the commands of the Great Commission from Matthew 28, and were challenged for a personal commitment, they prayed earnestly, asking God to show how they could be involved.

Few young people in this country remain on the farm as most migrate to urban areas to seek factory jobs or better educational opportunities. However, there were some young men attending the missions conference who had remained on the farm to assist aging family members not able to keep up the rigors of their daily chores. As participants understood the mandate of what Scripture says about the Great Commission, one young man named Brother Lee* shared that he was sensing a personal call to get involved. He was especially moved when he learned there were several unreached and unengaged people groups living in farming communities in the mountains in the southeastern part of the country—communities similar to where he had grown up and lived his entire life. To engage these farming communities, it would take someone who understood that lifestyle and could live in that rural environment, willing to work on farms to earn a living. This description moved Brother Lee's heart. He felt the missionary job profile shared in the meeting was a personal description of his life, and he interpreted this as God's call for him to be a missionary. Conference organizers prayed individually with Brother Lee, asking for the Father's will to be confirmed and clarified in the days ahead.

The following morning all participants were anticipating the last session of the conference. During breakfast, conference leaders looked for Brother Lee, hoping he could share a testimony with the conference participants of how the Lord was speaking to him regarding the unreached and what his calling might entail. But Brother Lee was nowhere to be found. When organizers asked a friend if he had seen Brother Lee, the friend told them that Brother Lee had left that morning. He was heading to the mountains to share the gospel with the unreached people group he felt the Lord had laid on his heart the day before. Everyone was shocked at this development. Brother Lee's passion for where he felt God was leading him overtook his understanding of the preparation he needed to fulfill that calling. Sadly, Brother Lee did not last very long on the mission field; he was home within a month.

FIRST THINGS FIRST

A DEEP STUDY OF SCRIPTURE often ignites a passion for the lost and motivates people to be willing to leave their familiar life and engage those who are much different in a faraway land. Passion, though, is not enough. Passion must be tempered with a process to clarify the calling in one's life and ensure all the elements are in place for effective, sustained missionary service. Additionally, a passion for the lost may not mean a calling to be a cross-cultural missionary or a calling to move one's family to a faraway location. It could be fulfilled in other ways such as financially supporting missions, praying for missionaries, and serving the missions cause in one's own community. It is important for a church to come alongside those who sense a call to serve as cross-cultural missionaries, mentor them each step of the way, and help them determine the specifics of the calling and how the calling can best be fulfilled.

Nobody had anticipated that Brother Lee would head off to engage in missions the day after he first sensed the call. We, as conference leaders, may have done a good job of communicating the urgency of getting the gospel to the lost, and especially to those who have never heard. But we had not clearly shared the need of the process to clarify the call, determine what preparation was needed, and then to complete the preparation before embarking on the journey of cross-cultural missions. While the mission is urgent, that does not eliminate the need to take the necessary time to prepare.

Many churches share they feel unprepared to mentor potential missionaries. This is especially a challenge for those churches with little or no cross-cultural experience. However, there are tools that churches can use to support and encourage those being called, as they walk together through this process of understanding God's call and determining the best way to be obedient to his calling. No individual or couple should walk through this experience in isolation. It should be done in community, allowing the church's strength to serve these members as they seek help to confirm and direct their call.

FROM WITHIN THEIR MIDST

CHURCHES CAN INTENTIONALLY raise up missionaries for service. As pastors cast the vision of the Great Commission and provide opportunities for service and ministry, the Lord will call out some members to leave home and engage the lost in other locations. Churches should encourage those interested in exploring their gifts and their calling to missions. This is best accomplished through mentoring relationships and studying Scripture to understand the missions calling. One must also understand the Missionary Task (see Step Eight), the requirements for each missionary role, and what role might best match a member's preparation and gifting.

It is important to remember that God's Word lays a foundation for missions, and when studied in community, people will better understand their calling, and be able to count the cost and prepare for what is ahead. The *Eight Steps* consultancy outlines five Bible studies that facilitate this process. When it is time to affirm candidates for service, church leaders are then in a good position to make informed recommendations, having been a part of this mentoring process.

These five Bible studies (see Appendix) provide a platform for candidates to consider key aspects of missions service in community. Although these studies are not necessarily written with only missionaries in mind, the topics cause one to prayerfully consider the implications of missions and the impact on comforts, family, and other aspects of one's life. The topics include:

- The Call to Missions
- The Command of Cross-Cultural Missions
- The Character of a Missionary
- The Life of a Missionary
- The Work of a Missionary

The Call to Missions. As Andrew Tuttle explains in "God's Call to Ministry",[9] the call to cross-cultural missions is not a single event but a progression of callings. Too often when individuals experience a spiritual high, as did Brother Lee when he literally packed his bags and headed for the mountains, people feel that the ultimate calling is the call to missions. In the first Bible study we emphasize that the ultimate calling is the fulfillment of the purpose the Lord has for an individual's life. If that purpose leads to overseas service, then we want to affirm and celebrate that direction. On the other hand, if the calling is to work a secular job and serve in the local church, being salt and light to the lost in an individual's community, we should celebrate that just as much.

Therefore, this first Bible study explores seven areas of calling in one's life, beginning with the initial calling—the call to salvation. The review of key passages such as Romans 3:23, Romans 6:23, John 3:16-17, and John 1:12, provides the opportunity for believers to affirm their status before the Lord, confirming that they came to the Lord in repentance and faith as the apostle Paul reflected in Romans 10:9-10. There have been times when people have never really examined their own salvation, something that they must confirm before exploring a calling to cross-cultural service. Whether or not a believer ends up serving as an overseas missionary, covering this key point is critical.

---

9. Andrew Tuttle, "God's Call to Ministry" (DMin diss., California Graduate School of Theology, 1987).

The second area of calling has to do with understanding the role Christians play in God's plan of reconciling mankind to himself (2 Corinthians 5:17-19). We have a role in bringing others to Christ so that they can also be reconciled to the Lord. He does the work, but he has given his people—his church—a ministry of reconciliation as we relate to a lost world. Before believers can consider moving to another land to minister to those in another culture, they must recognize the opportunity and responsibility to be salt and light to the nations living around them (Matthew 5:13-14), embracing the ministry of reconciliation as mentioned in 2 Corinthians. This may require a challenge to be involved in this ministry; it may also reveal the need for training and equipping for individuals to be able to share Christ with whomever the Lord brings into their path. When the Bible study is done in community, the church should be ready to step in and provide the training and mentoring to help believers be effective witnesses.

The third area of calling is service in the local church. Scripture tells us that the Lord equips every believer with spiritual gifts. It is the responsibility of church leadership to help believers discover their spiritual gifts and identify ways to use those gifts in service in the local church (Romans 12:1-8, 1 Corinthians 12:1-31). This lesson will challenge church leaders to fulfill their responsibility of equipping the saints (Ephesians 4:11-13). This may take time as believers test their gifting in various ministries, but there should be a clear understanding of how the Father has shaped them for service. The review of the spiritual gifts mentioned in Scripture can identify constructive ways to confirm and practice spiritual gifts in service through the local church.

These first three callings are important for every believer. The study in community can be beneficial to any new believer—anyone seeking to learn more about how they can follow the Lord in obedience and faith.

As we consider the fourth area of calling, the call to cross-cultural missions, we explore a more specific calling the Lord may have placed on an individual's life. This could mean sharing the gospel with another language group, ethnicity, or some other cultural perspective. It may mean stepping out of a place of familiarity and ease and learning to enter a world that is different and uncomfortable.

This calling doesn't necessarily mean moving to another country, or even away from one's home. In fact, this calling can almost always be fulfilled in one's own community, especially in major urban centers. Surprisingly, few local churches have understood or recognized this opportunity for ministry, though many diverse peoples live nearby in their own communities. Someone must take the gospel to them so that they can hear and understand. This type of cross-cultural ministry was reflected in the previous chapter with the story of the church pastor who discovered a Muslim reading room and community near his own church. The opportunity for cross-cultural ministry was essentially next door.

The fifth area of calling explored is the calling to leave home and things familiar to move to a place in need of a gospel witness (Romans 10:13-15). Ephesians 4:11 specifies that the Holy Spirit calls some to serve as "apostles," or "sent ones." To fulfill this calling requires these individuals to move away from home to take the gospel to unreached peoples and places. With thousands of unreached people groups remaining, the Great Commission cannot be fulfilled without many believers accepting the calling of the Lord to move themselves or their families to another place, learn the local language and culture, and plant their lives among the unreached to provide an incarnational witness for the sake of the gospel.

The sixth area of calling is the affirmation by the local church (Romans 10:11-15, Acts 13:1-3). The Christian life is designed to be lived in community and major decisions should be made in that community. The study of these lessons in community allows for the missionary candidate and others in the church to process these important decisions together. Therefore, just like the church in Antioch, it is important for the local church to seriously take on this responsibility. Although Paul and Barnabas had a specific calling from the Holy Spirit, the church prayed and fasted, laying on hands and praying for them before they were sent out. As the church in Antioch took the sending responsibility seriously, so should the church today in order to fulfill Romans 10:13-15.

The seventh calling is sensitive in many circles, but nevertheless must be addressed when a married couple is considering missionary service. A

husband and wife must be in harmony with the expression of their calling as they consider moving to a new location for the sake of the gospel
(Ephesians 5:21-33). The husband and wife may have different roles on
the mission field determined by gifting and opportunity. But they must
be in agreement with what the Lord has for them as a couple and understand that they are in this endeavor together as a family. While not always
the case in some missions-sending circles, the IMB appoints both husband and wife as missionaries. Christian families can greatly impact local
cultures as they model how a Christian family is different from others.
Furthermore, in many cultures it is only appropriate for women to share
the gospel with women, and men with men. Therefore, considering gifting
and family needs, both husband and wife must sense a calling of the Lord
to serve and be equipped as cross-cultural workers. In our experience as
missionary candidate assessors, we have seen that when the husband and
wife are not in unity, the gospel witness is often compromised and presence on the mission field is rarely sustained.

The call of God should be evident in the life of every believer, but that
does not mean that every believer is called to leave family and home to be
a cross-cultural missionary. Therefore, the calling to serve as a cross-cultural missionary should be carefully assessed by working through these
seven areas of calling in community, recognizing the stage of life and other
factors that may impact where the Lord might have the believers serve.

The Command of Cross-Cultural Missions. This Bible study focuses on
Acts 10 and looks at how the Lord began to break the Jewish disciples out
of their ethnocentric approach to ministry and reveal to them the enormous world of the Gentiles, who needed the gospel. This experience
served to demonstrate to the apostle Peter that God's plan truly did mean—
as stated in the Matthew 28:19-20 version of the Great Commission—all
peoples. Peter needed this vision to fully understand that God included
all Gentiles in his redemptive plan, and even those who were part of the
occupying Roman government.

The Bible study challenges participants regarding their own prejudices
and willingness to move from the comfort of their own lives and culture to

enter another that will feel foreign and quite possibly uncomfortable. The study will confirm their calling to move in this direction or raise concerns or issues that must be addressed before deciding about missions service.

The Character of a Missionary. The third Bible study in the series reviews passages from Romans 12 and Philippians 2:1-5. The study summarizes and contrasts between good and bad character traits and connects spiritual gifts with service to others in the church. We recognize there is nothing in this passage that specifies the requirements for a missionary. The key is to understand that a missionary must be of the highest character, reflecting the characteristics of Christ. This is the standard the Lord has for his followers as reflected in many portions of Scripture. The Bible study serves as an opportunity to conduct a personal assessment and identify areas for possible growth.

The Life of a Missionary. Sometimes people view the life of a missionary as an adventure during which everything works out just as planned. On the contrary, following Jesus, especially as a cross-cultural missionary, can lead to challenging and unanticipated experiences. In Matthew 8:18-27, Jesus issued a call for people to follow him. Many expressed a willingness to do so, but Jesus' interactions with them tested their commitment and motivation. We need to ask ourselves the same questions today.

This Bible study explores three areas that intersect with the missionary life in ways that sometimes surprise new missionaries as they learn to live on the mission field. The first area is the loss of things familiar. Jesus challenged the scribe who wanted to follow him in Matthew 8:18-20, telling him that life would not only be different, but that it would be much less comfortable than the life to which he was accustomed. Living conditions, food, transportation, and even subtle aspects of missionary life such as sanitation, traffic, and noise—seemingly minor issues—can become major irritants when the pressures of cross-cultural stress take their toll.

The next two verses reflect the second area of impact, the potential consequences on family and family relationships (Matthew 8:21-22). In today's world, electronic communication resources allow families to stay in touch, even when separated by thousands of miles. But the challenges to family relationships can be much deeper. Missionaries, because of their distant places of service, often miss key family events such as weddings, births, and funerals. During times of family crisis, resentment can build because the missionary is not in the same country to assist other family members as they carry the load. Additionally, the children of missionaries often bond more closely with the culture they are growing up in rather than the home culture of their parents. This can cause them to seem distant to grandparents, uncles, and aunts.

It does not have to be this way. Missionaries can take advantage of opportunities to keep in touch with family in tangible ways such as remembering birthdays and holidays, and spending quality time when they do have the chance to be with them back at home. One missionary shared that his mother actually felt closer to his child than her other grandchildren. That was because when they were able to be together, they spent significant time with each other and built a close bond. The child and the grandmother wrote each other regularly, exchanged pictures and stories, and shared life with each other, even though most of the time they were separated by thousands of miles.

For missionary families, the relationships with their extended families will change and could become tense, especially with those who do not understand the missionary call or consider the missions mandate as important. These challenges cannot be avoided, but the missionary and church family can be aware and take action to make the best of the situation. Most importantly, extended family members can be encouraged to embrace the Great Commission and their role as "senders," while the missionaries are the "sent ones." In "Planning for Cross-Cultural Missions" (Step Five), we encourage participants to list what it takes to be good senders and then develop action plans to begin fulfilling that responsibility.

Finally, this Bible study helps to flesh out the third area of major impact for missionaries: dealing with challenges that seem insurmountable. The storm faced by the disciples can represent many of the issues missionaries may confront on the field—overwhelming issues without easy answers. Just as the disciples marveled at the power of Jesus to control the elements, Matthew 8:23-27 reminds us of whom we serve, providing a benchmark of hope. The Lord we serve is the creator of the universe and residing in his hands is the best place to be, even in the midst of the storm. This passage gives hope to persevere through the challenging times, even when a resolution is not in sight.

"The Life of a Missionary" Bible study helps to flesh out these significant issues, but it also provides a benchmark of hope as expressed in Matthew 8:23-27. The Lord we serve is the creator of the universe and residing in his hands is the best place to be, even during the storms of life. This passage gives hope to persevere through challenging times.

The Work of a Missionary. This final Bible study is based on Acts 18 and 2 Timothy 2:1-3 and helps to look at the Missionary Task in the context of the first-century church as Paul and his band of missionaries took the gospel to much of the known world of his day. Paul worked to multiply his efforts as he enabled and trained others. The passage also provides the opportunity to discuss and contrast the role of the missionary with that of a pastor. There are many skills that parallel one another, but the missionary has to keep the full Missionary Task in mind with the vision to move toward the stage of Exit to Partnership with intentionality.

Raising up missionaries is possible for any congregation if it is intentional. Essentially, a church is discipling believers to understand and fully embrace their calling. Working through that process in community is an important part of the discipleship process. As we will discuss in "Selecting and Training Cross-Cultural Missionaries" (Step Six), the goal is to help all believers be in the right place at the right time, using the gifts the Lord has given them. In a few cases, that will be serving as a cross-cultural missionary and moving a family to a different location to fulfill that call. In most cases, it will mean engaging in work near one's home, in either a ministry setting or secular work, and living as salt and light in a lost world (Matthew 5). When a Christian discovers that place of service—regardless of where it is—it is a time of celebration for all.

6

STEP FIVE

Planning for Cross-Cultural Missions

T HE CHURCH HAD GROWN tremendously in recent years on the island nation of Madagascar, a country with nearly 27 million people. Church planting in the populous southern part of the island had accelerated, and as a result of this ten-year expansion, believers there were sensing God's call and their responsibility to share the gospel with others who had never heard. They were especially concerned about the unreached people living in isolated areas of the island's north, separated from the south by the rugged Tsaratanana mountain range. Beyond these mountains there was little infrastructure to promote development, transportation, and communication.

A group of leaders in the Malagasy Baptist Convention began to pray and consider how they might lead their churches and convention to fulfill this calling. Through their relationship with IMB missionaries working in Madagascar, they reached out to us, the IMB globalization team, to come to their island to help them look at ways they could become effective senders, hoping to deploy their own Malagasy missionaries to this unreached area.

Not long after we arrived on this Indian Ocean island, we climbed into a Missionary Aviation Fellowship single-engine Cessna to survey the northern part of the island and assess the status of Christianity and the church there. Two IMB missionaries and three Malagasy convention partners accompanied us as we flew to locations they considered representative of the north. Roads were impassable at the time because of recent rains, but the plane made it possible to drop into these locations. As we approached the dirt airstrips in the north, the MAF pilot circled to alert local farmers that we were preparing to land. The farmers would then drive their cattle off the runways so that we could touch down on our second approach. At each place—market centers and settlements with larger populations—we first visited the local police stations to inform them of our presence. Foreigners rarely visit these towns.

The areas proved to be not only economically depressed, but it was clear that the church growth in the southern part of the island had not influenced these remote northern locations. Instead, we found evidence of animism, ancestor worship, and the burden of the fear of spirits and demons. Local inhabitants had placed protective charms, amulets, and small objects, items meant to appease evil spirits, in homes and in trees. The few Christians we discovered told us about the animism practices and recognized the spiritual need of the people. Even a non-Christian local official shared that the people needed Christian missionaries to impact the development of society in a positive way. Perhaps most importantly, the few believers that we discovered could be a foundation for future churches to be planted. Those same believers, however, expressed a need for leadership to help them grow in the Lord and to understand how to be a part of a new church plant.

The week following the tour, 300 delegates at the annual convention of Malagasy Baptists heard our findings from the survey trip. During that meeting, members of the convention overwhelmingly approved selecting a committee of ten men to explore how best to get this missions endeavor under way.

A few months later, the convention invited us back to lead an *Eight Steps* consultation to help them realize their vision. During the consultation, we explored each of the *Eight Steps* with the convention's missions committee, a representative group of convention leaders and their spouses, and three IMB missionary families based in Madagascar. During the honest and free-flowing discussion, challenges surfaced regarding each of the steps, yet the group resolved to keep seeking the Lord's guidance to move forward. The focus of the group returned to the original question: "What is God's heart for the people of Madagascar, especially those in the north?"

As they sought the answer, the group focused on a time of concentrated prayer and read related Scriptures. They discussed the diverse language and cultural backgrounds of the Malagasies in the north who lived in communities with little or no access to the gospel. Then, on a large piece of butcher paper taped to the wall, they drew an outline of the island, plotting the known evangelical churches. The map revealed very few churches in the northern half of the island. This lack of gospel witness there brought them to their knees in prayer, asking the Lord for guidance and direction.

After this time of prayer, reading God's Word, and reflection, the group resolved to move forward by creating a plan with specific action steps. They selected a small task force and determined initial actions, such as developing and distributing prayer resources to churches. These pointed out the lostness in the north and provided specific requests for churches to begin praying through. This information included population numbers by region, false religions the unreached Malagasies followed, and the limited access to the region and the gospel. The prayer resources also pointed out the need for the Lord to call "workers into his harvest" as Jesus commanded in Matthew 9:37-38.

The task force was asked to investigate government employment opportunities that might provide income for Malagasy missionaries sent from the churches to this underserved area of the island. They planned for additional survey trips as well. By the time the group left the room, they were convinced that the Lord would provide what was needed to fulfill their calling to send missionaries to this neglected part of the island of Madagascar.

Hebrews 11:6 tells us that "...without faith it is impossible to please God...." The overwhelming consensus of the group in Madagascar was that they needed to step out in faith to follow the leading of the Holy Spirit, trusting the Lord to provide. Therefore, they developed some simple, yet measurable action steps to get started:

1. They selected a small group to flesh out their plan.
2. They began distributing prayer information to churches.
3. They established a task force to explore opportunities for employment for potential missionaries in the northern part of the island.
4. They explored opportunities to conduct additional survey trips to visit remote, unreached segments of the island.

MOVING FORWARD

MANY CHURCHES AND PASTORS may feel limited in their potential to be involved in missions due to church size or economic limitations. However, even a small church can make a significant contribution to the missions enterprise. Each church must do what it can and what the Lord places on its members' hearts. If missions is at the core of a church's vision, the Lord will provide direction and resources. To make progress, however, the church must have a plan that creates visible action steps to invite and encourage full participation of its congregation, whether the members are "senders" or "goers." A comprehensive plan is necessary for the church to send and sustain missionary presence. The churches in Madagascar had little missions experience. However, they utilized the help of IMB missionaries based in their country, the IMB globalization team's *Eight Steps* consultancy, the study of Scripture, and prayer to intentionally move forward as they embraced the missions vision the Holy Spirit had placed on their hearts. One important observation is that the Malagasy initiative was not generated by "outsiders," although IMB missionaries and the consultancy team provided input and advice. The Malagasy Baptist Convention created its own plan after seeking the Lord's direction and studying the Word, combined with working through the content of the *Eight Steps of the Missions Continuum*. Particularly important for this group was understanding the scope of the Missionary Task and "The Six Critical Questions" of Church Mobilization found in Step Two (see pages 26-30).

BEGINNING THE PROCESS

WE RECOMMEND that a church begin its missions-sending process with the five fundamental actions listed on the following page. Some of these are addressed in previous chapters such as becoming a healthy church in which all members are using their spiritual gifts in service to the church. Additionally, the church needs to identify how to raise awareness about all levels of ministry, from local ministry in the community to cross-cultural missions that reaches beyond borders and even to foreign countries. We also recommend a small group or committee to consider the scope of details in becoming a missions-sending church, involve the entire church in the effort, and honor the privacy of individuals or couples who may be exploring serving as missionaries. Finally, the church should develop action steps to put the process in motion. These include raising funds, developing partnerships, and considering the implications of supporting missionaries both financially and spiritually for the long term.

BECOMING A MISSIONS-SENDING CHURCH

Fundamentals of becoming a missions-sending church are:

1. Equip all church members to serve the church by utilizing their spiritual gifts (Ephesians 4:11-12). Engaging members in service in the church is the first step in identifying potential missionaries.
2. Prepare the church by actively becoming an Acts 1:8 church. This begins with a recognition of lostness surrounding the church—its "Jerusalem." It moves to local cross-cultural ministry (as in "Samaria," an area that was near but culturally different from traditional Jews). "Judea" signifies reaching out to a larger area, state, or province—and people with similar or different cultural backgrounds. And finally, "to the ends of the earth."
3. Establish a decision-making group that will develop a thorough knowledge of missions. They will then work with the church to develop a plan of action to involve all aspects of missions-sending as the Lord provides the opportunity.
4. Involve the entire church in the implementation of the plan, from the youngest children to the senior adults.
5. Develop a plan for missions involvement that includes these elements:

    □   Pray for a specific unreached people group in the community and elsewhere in the world.
    □   Provide opportunities for cross-cultural ministry, locally and beyond, to the extent possible.
    □   Develop a plan to raise funds for missions endeavors.
    □   Use the experience and expertise of a missions-sending agency or missions-sending committee of the convention when possible, especially in terms of prayer promotion.
    □   Work closely with a missions-sending agency that can provide expertise in missionary assessment. Empower a small review team to assess the readiness of missionary candidates. This group will maintain the confidentiality of the missionary candidates but ensure there has

been a thorough assessment for the benefit of not only the church, but also the candidates and the field. (Also see "Developing Partnerships," Step Seven.)

□ When your church prepares to send long-term missionaries, develop a plan for their continued support and encouragement while they are serving. This plan may include regular communications with church representatives and occasional visits and cooperating mission trips. It may also include providing encouragement and assistance for extended family members, such as aging parents, not moving with them to the mission field.

In Madagascar, developing a plan to involve all the churches in the convention in cross-cultural missions happened relatively quickly. It only took about one year from the initial survey trip to receiving the convention's endorsement and initiating the task force action plans. This is at least in part because missionaries and local pastors were praying to this end; before the actual process started, the vision was beginning to take shape in their hearts and minds. Many of the convention church representatives were on board and awaiting the right time to move forward. The fact that the mission field was actually in the same country simplified some of the logistics.

PUTTING A MISSION-SENDING PLAN IN MOTION

IN CONTRAST, it took about three years for the Eastern Baptist Convention of Cuba to build an effective missions-sending plan. At the beginning of the process, leaders of the Eastern Baptist Convention knew that it was time to begin planning in earnest to send their own missionaries to the nations. They had attempted to send missionaries in previous years, but those attempts had faced insurmountable obstacles in coordination, funding, and travel restrictions.

With an IMB relationship already in place, the president of the convention invited us to Cuba as the IMB globalization team to help develop a strategy to recruit and send convention-sponsored Cuban missionaries to the nations. The entire convention leadership attended the first meeting. At that meeting, the leaders shared their vision of what they felt God wanted them to do: to first send missionaries to plant churches among close-culture, Spanish-speaking unreached peoples, and then later to branch out to other languages and people groups.

The president of the convention of churches had a passion for seeing the gospel spring forth from Cuba to the nations; however, he knew that neither he nor this group of leaders were the ones who needed to be making plans and decisions in this effort. The convention leaders recognized the importance of having the right people making decisions about how to send missionaries, and more importantly, whom to send. This would require a small group of individuals concentrating on the specific tasks related to selecting and sending qualified missionaries. Convention leaders prayed and discussed how to move forward, recognizing they must address many challenges to finally see Cuban missionaries successfully deployed to the mission field.

Since the convention already had a network of missions directors, the convention president charged the national director of missions with recruiting and organizing an international missionary selection team. To be part of the newly formed team, each member needed to demonstrate a passion for missions, but also needed a certain expertise to add to the skillset of the group. The team included the missions directors who represented the churches in each geographic region. It also needed a number of specialists such as a theologian to help assess and develop the theological soundness of the missionary candidates, and a physician and a Christian psychologist to determine the physical and emotional wellness of candidates. A professor from the Baptist Theological Seminary of Eastern Cuba filled the role of the team's theologian, and a Spanish language professor from the same seminary was appointed to help develop the missionary application materials. The national missions director also recruited his own secretary, who was gifted in administration and organization, to manage the written application materials of potential candidates.

Once they identified the members, the group needed practice in processing applicants. As the consultancy team, we held subsequent meetings with them to help them organize their application forms. We also helped them practice skills such as reviewing applications, conducting interviews, and evaluating job opportunities. The group determined their own decision-making processes regarding missionary applicants, while at the same time honoring the confidentiality of the applicants' information.

As mentioned before, this process took time—approximately three years before it was thoroughly established, rehearsed, and implemented by convention leaders. The Eastern Baptist Convention of Cuba developed a process that not only addressed all of the foundational issues related to the sending of cross-cultural missionaries, but one that is also uniquely Cuban, both structurally and culturally. This is the intent of the *Eight Steps* process. With the principles in place, sending churches and agencies can make contextualized plans to effectively establish missions sending from churches in any cultural setting to the mission field.

PRACTICAL CONSIDERATIONS

AS A CHURCH TAKES STEPS to move forward with intentionality, there are areas of consideration which impact where it sends missionaries. These could include the prospective missionary's experience in different components of the Missionary Task, languages needed to communicate effectively, and qualifications required for a specific job. In other cases, there may be practical challenges to figure out how to get things done while taking into consideration limitations of communication, transport, children's needs, and access. When needed, partnerships with established agencies or other missionary teams already on the ground can be developed to help in many areas where the infrastructure—such as logistical help to find housing and transportation—is not available or feasible to develop.

Fundraising is always a concern with missions endeavors. Churches and agencies may recognize approaches to fundraising that include various avenues of funding such as direct support, project funding, cooperative giving, and business as mission. It may be that one source of funding is not adequate and churches or networks must develop a combination of funding sources. At any rate, the rationale for raising funds for missions must be communicated to the church along with the need to support missionary families who leave their homes to share the gospel in another location. This must also include providing them with financial resources to carry out the Missionary Task.

With fundraising, there needs to be a level of vigilance regarding how funds are to be used on the mission field. Accountability processes must be in place to provide appropriate reports to donors. Missiological implications are worth investigating to address key issues such as sustainability, reproducibility, and dependency. Churches must also grapple with the challenge of establishing work that multiplies itself, which includes the discipline of stewardship in the local church.

One responsibility that often evades new missions-sending entities is the need for missionary care. Missionary families encounter challenges on the field and need ongoing support and prayer, as well as pastoral and even clinical care at times. The development of appropriate partnerships can help in this area, especially if a church or agency lacks resources or expertise. However, even a small church can maintain contact with its missionaries, providing regular prayer, encouragement, and remembering them during special times of the year such as birthdays, holidays, and during times of grief or loss. It is important that the whole church, as seen in the chapter on "Church Mobilization" (Step Two), carefully considers the support needs of missionaries and participates in the delivery of services to these families. The missionary care plan is not standard for every case, but depends on the access, resources, and expertise of each contributor. This is an area in which good communication from the sending church can serve missionaries well, especially those deployed to remote and difficult places. When the partnerships with churches, networks, and sending organizations work well, missionaries benefit greatly as their needs are effectively and efficiently met.

As we mentioned, Hebrews 11:6 states, "Now without faith it is impossible to please God, since the one who draws near to him must believe that he exists and that he rewards those who seek him." Missions sending is no different. We cannot wait until we have all the resources we need to begin. God often provides the resources as we step out in faith. The churches of Madagascar and Cuba are great examples. They still have enormous challenges and needs that have yet to be resolved locally. However, they have begun the process by making plans and moving forward as God provides the resources. It seems that the more they pray and act in obedience to the Lord's direction, the straighter the path becomes, overcoming barriers to the unreached. Let that be a testimony to us all as we apply the truth given to us in Hebrews 11:6.

7

STEP SIX

Selecting and Training Cross-Cultural Missionaries

A MEGACHURCH in an affluent Southeast Asian city was struggling. The church members and leadership had always thought of their church as "missions minded," yet they had little vision for sending long-term missionaries. Church members gladly gave money to support short-term mission trips and human needs projects, but somehow they had not caught the vision for long-term missions: individuals or families investing their lives among unreached peoples, learning language and culture, sharing the gospel, and starting churches.

The church leaders invited our team to present the *Eight Steps of the Missions Continuum* consultancy. As they began to work through the material, God's heart for the nations became evident to them throughout Scripture. One leader confessed, "We have just been playing missions. It is now time to get serious." They recognized that the church's two or three annual mission trips were not adequately embracing the Great Commission that God gave the church. Something needed to change.

The study of God's Word helped the church leaders understand that to make a sustaining impact on global lostness, they needed to consider long-term presence in the places they had been working. Up until this time, they had successfully engaged human needs projects in foreign countries through short-term trips. During these trips, church members shared the gospel through tracts or through translators. But there was never a strategy to follow up or plant a church. Short-term teams were beneficial in casting vision for the participants and mobilizing church members to pray, but these trips did not provide a sustained missionary presence among the people they engaged during those brief weeks each year. They realized they needed a continual presence on the mission field: church-sent missionaries planting their lives and planting churches.

In order for their church to send long-term missionaries to provide this ongoing presence, however, they realized that they needed to identify the church members God might be calling into long-term service; they understood that motivation and mission-trip experience were not enough to identify those individuals. They also recognized the need within the church to be more intentional in raising up missionaries. Thus, the church developed a plan to organize potential missionaries into cohorts to review and discuss the Bible studies from "Raising up Missionaries" (Step Four).[10] Additionally, during the consultation, we introduced the leadership to Five Components of Missionary Assessment to help them understand how to send the right people to the right place at the right time, as previously discussed in the Missionary Task chapter. In many cases, churches or agencies identify the right person, but the candidate needs further preparation to meet the unique requirements of the mission field.

To help a church or organization thoroughly assess missionary

---

10. The five Bible studies discussed in "Raising Up Missionaries" can be found in the Appendix.

candidates, we have grouped areas of a missionary's life into five components. As you read through the components, it's important to understand that the process must be thorough, and the church or agency assessment team selected for this task must be trustworthy and honor confidences.

FIVE COMPONENTS OF MISSIONARY ASSESSMENT

Component 1 — Christian and Church Identity

Assessing candidates' lives in terms of Christian and church identity helps determine the right person. Not only does the assessment team need to understand these facets of a candidate's life, but candidates need to evaluate themselves as well, and determine which areas they need to strengthen. Just as in the discussion related to leadership development within the Missionary Task, in this assessment, we look at the same three areas: Who the missionary candidates are to BE, what they are to KNOW, and what they are to DO.

Who is a missionary to BE? This facet has to do with a candidate's Christian character. Missionaries should first be believers in Jesus and able to clearly voice their Christian testimony. In addition, their lives should be a testimony displaying the characteristics of Christ. Other people should recognize them as persons of high character and the local church must affirm candidates for missionary service. The church members should see evidence of missionary candidates having healthy relationships with others, both inside and outside the church. Ultimately, the prospective missionaries should be examples of individuals being transformed by the Holy Spirit, allowing God to impact every aspect of their lives.

What should a missionary KNOW? Missionaries should have a deep understanding and knowledge of the Bible and how to apply biblical principles to daily life. They should also have deep convictions related to the authority of God's Word. They should regularly study God's Word on their own and be involved in teaching sound doctrine within their local church. They should have a clear biblical understanding of Christian doctrines, such as believer's baptism, the Lord's Supper, and the doctrine of the Trinity: God the Father, God the Son, and God the Holy Spirit. Furthermore, they should have a solid understanding of the nature of sin, the character of God, salvation, and basic ecclesiology as taught by the local church and affirmed by the larger body of Christ, such as a sending organization.

What should a missionary DO? What ministry skills do they possess and what visible witness do they have in the community which reflects their inner character? Missionaries' actions must be consistent with a clear Christian testimony. They must have followed in obedience to the Lord's command for believer's baptism and participate in the Lord's Supper on a regular basis as practiced in the local church. They should model sound Christian disciplines which include individual and corporate prayer, personal and corporate Bible study, and using their spiritual gifts in service through the church.

This first component combines one's Christian identity with one's identity in the local church. Together, these emphasize that Christians do not live lives in isolation but in the supportive context of the local body of believers. Therefore, the prospective missionary's Christian identity should be visible and demonstrated in the local church.

Component 2 — Confirming the Missionary Call

The "Call to Missions" Bible study presented in Step Four is designed to assist missionary candidates and the local church in exploring the various aspects of the Christian calling. It also helps candidates to clarify the specifics of their call, especially if they are considering moving a family to another country to serve as cross-cultural missionaries. Candidates working through this process in the community of the local church allow for the body of Christ to provide direction, prayer, consultation, and affirmation as the specifics of the calling become clear. As we wrote in "Raising Up Missionaries," the church at Antioch took the sending of Paul and Barnabas seriously. They knew them well, as they had been with them for a significant time. The two men had proven themselves faithful in a short-term assignment of taking an offering to assist the church in Jerusalem. Still, the church prayed and fasted before sending them off on their mission, as the

Holy Spirit had instructed them.

Assessing the missionary call in this Step Six is somewhat different from the exploration of one's calling described earlier in Step Four. In Step Four, candidates work through seven different stages of calling to clarify the Lord's will for their lives. In this step, we are assessing if this prospective missionary is the right person that God has called to a particular role in ministry. If candidates are unsure of their calling, we encourage them to review the "Call to Missions" Bible study to work through this process.

Evaluating the Missionary Call

When evaluating a potential missionary's call, the assessor can focus on four categories of calling. Studying these categories can help determine how an individual's calling can be interpreted in terms of the life circumstances at a given time.

1. *Call to Salvation:* responding to the Lord's expression of grace in faith and repentance.
2. *Call to Mission:* essentially called to be a disciple of Christ and a disciple-maker.
3. *Call to Station:* various stations of life require us to serve the Lord in terms of the realities of our everyday lives, such as being a parent, or being married or single.
4. *Call to Service:* God has endowed each believer with gifts to serve the local body of believers—the local church. These gifts are not all the same, but one should know one's spiritual gifts and use those gifts in service to the local church.[11]

Realities Within the Call

We met Mae* at an Asian missionary training center. Mae had been preparing several years for overseas missions and was in the final

---

11. "Calling," in *Foundations* (Richmond, VA: IMB, 2018), 65-66.

stages of preparation when her father unexpectedly passed away. He had been the primary caregiver of her disabled mother. In Mae's home culture, it is the responsibility of the family to provide for family members needing special care. Mae was an only child and was devastated by her father's passing. His death also meant that her opportunity to deploy as a missionary would now be on hold, as she was now responsible to care for her mother. Considering these circumstances, she had difficulty reconciling the calling the Lord had placed on her heart. The Call to Station discussion gave Mae perspective. God could still use her as a missionary in due time, but now her station in life was to serve as the caregiver of her mother.

As we discuss the entire missions-sending process, we must balance the "three rights." In this case, Mae had the skills and preparation necessary for an overseas assignment and thus qualified as the right person. The right place had been identified as well, as her background was a good match to the needs of the mission field. Nevertheless, the right timing was not in alignment. Ultimately, Mae found that the Lord would use this time for her to be a gospel witness to those in her community as she cared for her mother. She learned to pray that the Lord would keep the missions calling on her heart and give her patience to serve well where she was.

⤙ Beyond Peoples and Places

There are times when missionaries sense a call that is specific to a place or people. This, however, can be disrupted when wars, natural disasters, or governmental restrictions prohibit missionaries from gaining access to those peoples or places where they desire to serve. While specific callings can and do happen, the exploration must be much deeper than just a place or people. It must be a submission to the will of the Lord, a willingness to follow his leading, even when the path changes due to unforeseen circumstances. In the book *Whom Shall We*

Send?[12] Andy Tuttle writes that a specific assignment may be temporary, but the call to be "on mission" with God is for a lifetime.

In the case of evaluating prospective missionaries who are married, the assessor must be willing to discuss the concept of calling with both the husband and wife. The "Call to Missions" Bible study mentions the necessity for a husband and wife to be in unity in their calling. Often, both may not feel called at the same time; one or the other may sense their calling first. It is important that each one shares that calling with his or her spouse, but this must be tempered with patience to allow the Lord to work in the other's life according to his own timing. The key is that the couple works in harmony, allowing time to address the questions and concerns either one may have.

One such couple was Frank* and Kay*. Frank felt a strong sense of calling to cross-cultural missions. Kay had expressed a sense of calling as a teenager and remembered having a keen interest in missions during childhood involvement in programs at her church. But in the midst of marriage, a busy career, a new baby, and the pressures of day-to-day life with a young family, this calling had faded. Kay was hesitant to voice her concerns as she did not want to quench the excitement Frank felt, but she could not share in his enthusiasm, though she was willing to be an obedient wife and go along.

As they discussed the possibility of serving as missionaries overseas, the topic grew uncomfortable as Frank's patience grew strained. During this time, at the advice of his pastor, Frank backed off and gave Kay time to work through and understand her hesitations—a process that ended up taking about three years.

Kay came to realize that she was concerned for her family that would be left behind in the US. She was also fearful of her son growing up and not knowing his grandparents well; she didn't want him to miss out on the special relationship she remembered having with her own grandparents during childhood years. In those three intervening years,

---

12. Andrew Tuttle, "Facets of a Call to Missions," in *Whom Shall We Send? Understanding the Essentials of Sending Missionaries,* ed. Joel Sutton (Richmond, VA: IMB, 2016), 71.

however, God showed her that he could care for her extended family, even if she was living thousands of miles away in a different country. God also provided assurance through the testimonies of other missionaries sharing how close their children were to grandparents. Most of all, the Holy Spirit calmed her heart with the promise in Philippians 4:19, that God would supply all her needs, including those of her family in the US and her son's on the mission field.

Looking back, Frank and Kay realized that God was doing something else during those three years. Through situations at work, Frank learned a lot about leadership, dealing with adversity, and working through conflict and difficult relationships. Although it was a challenging time, this experience and growth served him well when he encountered similar issues on the field and had the experience of having worked through those same issues in a biblical manner.

The assessment of calling is not a list of boxes that must be checked, or a study to be completed, but an endeavor of seeking the Lord in affirming and clarifying how individuals or couples are to live out their lives in obedience to the Father. As the church comes alongside missionary candidates, they can walk through this process together, supporting and encouraging each other as the Lord makes his will clear over time.

Component 3 — Missionary Competencies and Qualifications

Determining the right person for the right place requires us to consider the competencies and qualifications for a particular job on the mission field.

A *competency* is the ability to be successful or efficient at something. An example would be the ability to initiate a conversation to share the gospel with a lost person, or to teach a group of pastors the doctrine of salvation. Are the candidates competent in the activities necessary to implement the Missionary Task, such as sharing the gospel, discipling new believers, and training and equipping church leaders? One competency that may be necessary to assess will be the candidate's capacity to learn the target language.

A *qualification* is an accomplishment that makes a person suitable for the job, such as a medical degree if the job is related to a healthcare assignment. Today, many countries of the world no longer grant missionary visas. The missionary must have a skill or qualification to gain access and remain in the country. Another qualification may be a seminary degree that is necessary for the field assignment or for appointment by the sending church or agency. In some cases, an advanced degree such as a doctorate in biblical languages may be required to teach in a theological institution. There may be other areas of qualification that will allow the missionary to enter the country of assignment. This could be a college degree, verifiable professional experience, or other qualifications the country might value enough to grant a visa.

Component 4 — Missionary Health and Wellness

Christian and church identity, missionary call, and competencies and qualifications are all important aspects of missionary assessment and preparation. The goal is to match a missionary—the right person—to a ministry opportunity—the right place—based on the required skills and needs of the mission field. However, missionaries rarely leave the field because they arrived with the wrong competencies or qualifications for the job, or because of faulty theological beliefs. These aspects of the prospective missionary's life are easy to observe, verify, and assess. More often, missionaries have unfruitful ministries or must leave the field because of health and wellness issues. Therefore, it is important to look deeply into physical, spiritual, and emotional health in order to conduct a comprehensive assessment of the candidate's readiness to serve overseas.

In Philippians 2:25-30, Paul writes to the church at Philippi that he was sending their missionary, Epaphroditus, home because he became sick on the mission field. He needed to return home to restore his health and to relieve the burden that his illness was causing Paul and others. This situation describes a physical illness that limited the missionary's ability to remain on the field and carry out his assignment. If the missionary's physical health is not carefully evaluated prior to going to the mission field, the church may be exposing both the missionary and the team on the field to difficult circumstances.

Assessing the right place to send a missionary may involve researching how the environment may impact a missionary's health. Locations with extreme conditions can affect missionaries in ways they may not have previously experienced. Rosemary*, a single missionary from the US, was sent by her sponsoring agency to a people group high in the Andes Mountains of South America, 13,000 feet above sea level. She had never been to a place with such dramatic elevation and shortly after arriving in her new city, she developed altitude sickness. While she hoped that she would adjust in time, even after living at this altitude for several months, her body did not acclimate. Rosemary's health deteriorated until she was not able carry out her ministry. Finally, her sponsoring agency moved her to a location at a much lower elevation to restore her health. Not only did she recover, but she thrived in that lower altitude environment and was able to continue her ministry fruitfully and faithfully.

How could Rosemary's months of illness have been avoided? When extreme conditions are known to exist in a particular location, it may be worthwhile to have missionaries visit before making a permanent move to see how their bodies respond to those conditions. Had Rosemary been able to visit that high-altitude location before moving there, she may have become aware of her vulnerability to altitude sickness. Fortunately, in her case, the situation was resolved before she developed long-term health consequences. It was clear from her missionary assessment that Rosemary was the right person. Her church affirmed her call to cross-cultural missions, and the timing was right, but the high-altitude city was not the right place for her to serve.

Likewise, chronic health conditions may require medication and care that is not available in certain locations. Locations with dangerous levels of air pollution may be unsuitable for candidates suffering from severe asthma. Candidates with back issues may be at high risk of permanent injury if they are sent to assignments requiring constant traveling on rutted and jarring roads. It is important that we steward God's resources well to assess each missionary's health before deployment to assure they can do the work they intend to do and remain on the mission field.

There are conditions that may disqualify a candidate because the risk is too high for the individual and healthcare costs may place a heavy burden on the sending church and agency. Examples include Type I diabetes, organ transplant patients, ulcerative colitis, and those with a history of malignancies and cancer. Assessors should consult with medical professionals in these cases to protect the health of the candidate and to steward financial resources well.

Physical health can be assessed with examinations by physicians and medical tests. Emotional and psychological health are equally important in missionary assessment but are more difficult to assess. God created us as complicated creatures. We each have a mind, a will, and emotions that can be infected with lies. Sin can hinder our effectiveness. Furthermore, cross-cultural stress can reveal and worsen these inner illnesses. Therefore, it is important to screen well for emotional and psychological health.

One common example of an emotional wellness issue is unresolved past sexual abuse. For example, how might a woman who suffered sexual abuse as a child be affected if she is sent to work in a culture where women are openly or frequently abused? Other examples of inner illnesses are depression, anxiety, eating disorders, and trauma from past or ongoing experiences. Some lifestyle issues may be a result of sinful patterns in life such as alcoholism, drug use, pornography use, and inappropriate sexual behavior. These experiences do not necessarily disqualify someone from serving, but the assessment team must ensure these issues have been recognized and resolved before sending the missionary into a situation of high cross-cultural stress. Resolution means that candidates disclose any such issues, knowing and understanding their identity in Christ, and allowing God's grace to heal them. Often in these cases, a candidate should consult a professional Christian counselor to ensure resolution has occurred. Resolution sometimes takes weeks, months, and possibly even years, depending on the extent of the illness.

Two other areas of wellness that must be assessed are marriage health and single identity. A couple must be able to affirm that Christ is the foundation of their marriage and give evidence of healthy marital communication. Some churches and agencies require at least a year of marriage before sending recently married missionaries overseas. Candidates should be able to affirm they are meeting each other's physical needs and be united in their call to serve as missionaries.

Singles must have a healthy understanding of singleness and have worked through any past issues as a single. They must demonstrate contentment in their singleness, even if they are open to the possibility of marriage in God's timing.

One last area of a family's assessment is related to children. If a married couple has children that will be accompanying them to the mission field, an adequate assessment should reveal any developmental and educational issues that could impact the successful deployment of the family. In revisiting the Kramer* family's situation from the opening chapter on the Missionary Task, the Kramers had a 16-year-old daughter, Christy, who struggled in her language skills and social life after she arrived on the field. Because she did not have an environment in which she could make friends, she became depressed, and her family eventually had to return to the US to address her emotional needs. Families with adolescent and teenage children need to be carefully assessed and will need to be in a place where the children will have a chance to thrive.

Component 5—Practical Preparation

Lastly, we must consider several practical aspects in the missionary assessment process. The first area to consider is missionary financial support. There are many strategies for providing missionary support and a church needs to establish a clear plan before deployment to ensure the missionary family has adequate resources when on the mission field. In "Planning for Cross-Cultural Missions" (Step Five) we discussed funding and cautions related to fundraising. Lack of planning in this regard in the Kramer's situation resulted in the family being under-supported, which added further to the stress they were already experiencing in adjusting to the mission field.

Another practical consideration as we identify the right person is the capacity of the candidate to learn language. As with Mike Kramer in the first chapter, an undiagnosed hearing loss impacted his capacity to learn a tonal language and diminished his effectiveness on the field. Other factors could impact language learning as well: a missionary's age, the time necessary to achieve the desired level of competency, and the actual cost of language study.

We must assess family obligations in the process. Are there responsibilities that could impact the missionary's ability to remain on the field? The "Life of a Missionary" Bible study in the Appendix is a good reference to help the candidate understand the impact of serving on family relationships. Will the candidate have responsibilities to care for aging parents in the coming years? Do the candidates have a family business or own a home in their country of origin? Does the missionary or family have debt that they should resolve before deploying to the field?

The church or agency should explore citizenship and visa issues as well. Will the missionary qualify for a visa to enter the desired country? Does the candidate have the immunizations necessary to enter the country? Another rarer situation could be a prospective missionary that has a criminal record from the past that might disqualify the individual from entering some countries.

As a prospective missionary family considers the right place, the needs of the children must be considered. What are the developmental and educational needs of the children? What schools are available and are they affordable? Are the children able to receive an adequate education via one of the schooling options? Does the host country allow homeschooling, and if so, are the parents equipped to teach their children at home while carrying out their ministry effectively? It is even important for the family to consider long-range educational considerations, such as where children might attend college, so that the secondary education will adequately prepare them for meeting admission standards. This is more than deciding which university children might attend, but also considers what language of instruction will be used and the admission requirements of prospective colleges.

When we conducted the *Eight Steps* consultancy with the megachurch in Southeast Asia referred to at the beginning of this chapter, the consultancy revealed one area the church leadership had not considered:

the readiness of dependent children to move overseas. In addition to the church leadership coming to understand that they needed to assess the emotional maturity, health and wellness of prospective missionaries' children, they realized they needed to assess educational needs as well. Consequently, in one case within this church, parents and teachers discovered a child with some learning challenges. With this additional knowledge the missionaries were able to delay their deployment, thoroughly assess the issues, and develop and implement appropriate intervention plans. Once the parents adequately addressed the challenge, the family was able to deploy to the field. In this case, the right persons were identified, as well as the right place. However, the timing was not right to sustain their missionary presence. Later, church leaders acknowledged that attention to the assessment details helped identify issues that could have led to the family's resignation after only a few months on the field had they not been addressed beforehand.

Different issues can surface at any stage of missionary assessment. Therefore, a thorough assessment serves not only the church and the mission team on the field, but helps the family resolve issues so they will be fruitful and more likely to sustain their presence on the mission field.

DEVELOPING AN INDIVIDUALIZED PROCESS

SENDING THE RIGHT PEOPLE to the right place at the right time requires that the missionary assessment process be completed allowing adequate time to consider all five components of missionary candidate readiness. We cannot expect candidates to be perfect, but we should see them growing in their walk with the Lord and seeking to allow him to impact every aspect of their lives. A good measure of the spiritual maturity of the candidates is how they respond to honest, Christ-centered accountability, advice, and correction.

A critical aspect of the process is how churches will conduct assessments and who will be responsible to gather the application materials and conduct the interviews. As part of the *Eight Steps* consultation, we assist churches and agencies in developing an evaluation team and application process that matches the church's decision-making system and structure. The process can be approached in different ways, but always includes the gathering of adequate applicant information, incorporates in-person interviews, and requests references from people who know the candidates well. In this way the church or agency can create candidate profiles that address each of the five components of missionary assessment.

As mentioned before, this process must be thorough, and the assessment team must be trustworthy and honor confidences. The electronic and written materials must be kept in a secure place with only limited access by those charged with the responsibility to assess candidates. When no longer needed, keeping in mind the legal and policy requirements to retain data, the materials should be destroyed to ensure confidentiality and privacy for the candidates. Often private and sensitive issues surface over the course of the application process and care must be taken to honor the safeguarding of that information and confidence entrusted to the assessment team. The assessment process must look at the whole person, and essentially the whole family.

ONE ASSESSMENT STORY

ALL OF THESE COMPONENTS must be woven together when assessing a missionary candidate or family to build a sound profile. Assessors also need to use discernment even with references from people close to the prospective missionary to understand the context in which references are given. Let us consider the assessment process of Aaron* and Mary.*

Aaron and Mary came to faith as adults and quickly became involved in the local ministries of their church in the Midwest US city where they lived. Their spiritual maturity deepened quickly and before long they became ministry leaders in the church.

During that time, the church leadership had a vision to move several families from their congregation across the country to an unchurched region to plant a new church. Neither Aaron nor Mary had formal seminary training or church planting experience, but they were eager to be involved in this new work and volunteered to go as part of the team. Aaron had experience running a small family business and Mary was a kindergarten teacher, so they felt they had the credentials and skills to support their family in this new location.

After their move and as they assisted their team's church-planting efforts, Aaron saw an opportunity to start a small business in their new city. Mary had found work as a schoolteacher. With this income they anticipated being able to both support their family and make contributions to the church plant so they could soon call a pastor to serve full time. Any free time in Aaron and Mary's week was spent ministering to the community and leading people to Christ. Aaron was a skilled evangelist and Mary loved to disciple younger women.

After two years, Aaron's new business had grown so much that it started to consume his ministry hours. He decided that ministry was more important than the business, so he sold the company to two young men he had recruited and trained. Stepping away from running the business gave Aaron more time for ministry. Soon, Aaron saw an opportunity to start another local business that could generate revenue to further support the new church plant. Once again, his business prospered, and he was able to sell it for a handsome profit after training up the new owners.

Not long after he sold his second business, Aaron and Mary began to sense that the Lord was calling them to take the gospel to an unreached people group overseas. With the support of their original sending church, they applied with a US-based missions agency. As a part of the assessment process, the agency requested references from several people in the sending church who knew Aaron and Mary well.

One of the church members had reservations. "Aaron is a fine young man. He is a faithful Christian, husband, and father. But he has never pastored a church, and he doesn't stay at any one job for very long," the man said. This member cited that Aaron had moved around from job to job over the past few years. "He starts businesses and sells them when they get too big. Every couple of years he starts a new business, then sells it to his employees. Missionaries need to be able to stay in one place for a long time to pastor a church, don't they?"

What this well-meaning man did not understand is the difference between the missionary role and the more traditional role of a church pastor. He did not fully comprehend what it would take to serve as a missionary church planter in a hard-to-reach location where Christian workers are not welcome. What he saw as weaknesses in Aaron could actually be strengths, considering the overseas situation where Aaron and Mary felt called to serve.

This is an example of needing to look at the whole person to determine if a missionary candidate is a good fit for the job and to consider the context in which references are given. We evaluate all five components together to get the big picture of the candidate's life. Even though Aaron had never pastored a church, he was a gifted evangelist and disciple-maker. He also knew how to recognize leadership and empower others to lead. He could start something, make it successful, and leave it with skilled leaders before moving on to the next thing. Mary also was a gifted teacher and disciple-maker and had discipled several women in their church plant. She had developed many valuable missionary competencies as a schoolteacher as well as a new church planter. Aaron and Mary are good examples of possessing the competencies and qualifications that can be transferred to carry out the work of a missionary.

Ultimately, the missions agency sent Aaron and Mary as church planters targeting an unreached people group, and to date they have helped start several new churches and have trained leaders for each church they started.

In "Raising Up Missionaries" (Step Four), we studied the story of Paul in Acts 18, and 2 Timothy 2. By Paul's examples, we see the missionaries starting the work, raising up leaders, then having them join with him to go to the next unreached people or place. As Paul trained Timothy to raise up more workers for the task, he followed his own advice by equipping Priscilla and Aquila, who then equipped Apollos for ministry. As potential missionaries are assessed, we look for skills that can be transferred and can contribute to the effective implementation of the Missionary Task. No one is perfect. No one has all the talents and abilities necessary. But God has given people experiences and abilities that are transferrable to the mission field. Those are the candidates that we attempt to identify who are the right people, whom we want to send to the right place at the right time.

8

STEP SEVEN

Developing Partnerships

M AIN STREET CHURCH,* a body of several hundred members in a southern US town, adopted the Mallakani* people who reside in a Southeast Asian country. Little information was available on the people group, but all indications suggested this people group only had a few believers and no churches or missions-sending agencies seeking to plant churches among them. The church began to pray for this people group and even sent a few teams overseas on survey trips to the area to learn about the local needs.

Bob and Jean Smith* were a part of the church's missions effort. Following a vision trip to the country, they felt God calling them to devote their lives to the Mallakani as cross-cultural church planters. Bob and Jean shared this calling with the church and after a period of prayer and assessment, the church agreed to send and support them as their missionaries to this unreached people. The church had little experience in sending missionaries so they connected with a missions-sending agency that could provide logistics infrastructure, strategy planning, and field support for the Smith family.

The Smiths learned the language well and were able to settle in a location in the heart of the Mallakani people group. They worked there on a tourism platform visa provided by the missions-sending agency. Bob spent about eight hours a week on platform management in return for the visa. Ministry moved slowly during their first year on the field and just about the time they began to gain momentum in the work among the Mallakani people, the agency lost some key personnel in a nearby country who were attached to the same tourism platform.

The agency saw no solution but to inform the Smiths that they would need to move to the nearby country so they could manage the platform. Many missionaries in the region depended on this platform for their visas. Due to Bob's business background and his knowledge of platform operations gained through experience, he was the only one who could fill this role.

This abrupt change mandated by the missions agency disillusioned the Smiths because their people group did not live in the neighboring country. Their supporting home church leadership felt betrayed because they were not involved in this decision and were not given an opportunity to speak into the dilemma. The agency's view was that the Smiths must consider the greater good of the work, which sometimes means sacrifice.

The Smiths found themselves in the middle of a major disagreement between their sending church, which provided their financial support, and the missions agency that provided their field infrastructure and visa. The church leadership questioned whether they could even continue supporting missionaries who were not focused on the church's adopted people group.

In the excitement of initially establishing this relationship, the church, the agency, and the missionaries never worked out the structures and decision-making processes if such a situation should arise. Amid the crisis, emotions were intense, time was short, and it was difficult to appropriately work through the issues with the various parties separated by oceans.

THE VALUE OF PARTNERSHIPS

THERE ARE FEW MISSIONARIES, churches, agencies, or teams on the field that have everything they need to effectively sustain their missions effort for the long term. Even large churches and agencies often need help in the missions enterprise. Carefully planned partnerships can provide this assistance. The *Eight Steps* process provides churches and agencies the opportunity to explore and understand the specific calling or vision for ministry they sense from the Lord, and then develop concrete action steps to move forward and fully embrace what the Lord has set before them. Part of this process includes identifying the types of partners and partnerships necessary to help fill in any gaps to fulfill that vision. These relationships, however, must be carefully thought through; some start out quite amicably, but conflict can erupt when unanticipated events occur that do not fit the original partnership agreement.

Prudent churches and agencies recognize the experience, expertise, and access that other like-minded groups can provide for the implementation of the Missionary Task. For example, let's review the positive results that came from a partnership with Cuban Baptists mentioned in Chapter One. In that situation, medical missionaries from Cuba joined an IMB team already functioning in Colombia. The partnership plan was for the Cuban missionaries to focus their energies on unreached villages in an indigenous reservation that Colombian government officials had not allowed missionaries from the US to access. The Cuban missionaries, because of their country of origin, medical training, and fluency in Spanish, were able to not only gain access, but also with their church-planting experience, were able to initiate Missionary Task activities in the area. Importantly, from the beginning, this partnership was one in which lines of authority and responsibility were carefully discussed, and the fruitful partnership emerged. The resulting partnership is fulfilling the vision of the IMB team, the Cuban missions-sending church, and the Cuban Baptist convention.

Most of all, it is seeing the Missionary Task effectively implemented in a previously unreached area.

PARTNERSHIP CONSIDERATIONS

THE DEVELOPMENT OF PARTNERSHIPS may require a careful review of a church or agency's approach to missions, which may include issues such as authority, decision making, supervision, and funding. Sometimes it requires the delegation of authority and supervision to someone in another entity. It may require providing funds and other resources to the partnership and giving up control of the details of how these resources may be used. A partnership might also mean the relinquishment of the ability to make strategic decisions. Not all churches, agencies, and missionaries are ready to concede these points. With any agreement, careful and honest discussion must take place regarding these key areas before entering into a partnership.

Two other areas for careful consideration before agreeing to a partnership relate to missiology and theology. In the missiological realm, it is important to discuss and clarify the role of the missionary, the use of outside funding, perspectives of dependency and reproducibility, and missionary methods. Likewise, entities considering a partnership should explore theological foundations which include views of basic doctrine, ecclesiology, biblical authority, church leadership, and the ordinances of the church, to mention a few. For most Baptist churches, the "Baptist Faith and Message"[13] is the standard document for agreement. Yet, even within Baptist circles, some churches express a more narrow theological view and potential conflicts can be avoided if these areas are clarified prior to entering into an agreement. It is important to understand one's own non-negotiables in these types of discussions, and also recognize areas where entities may have preferences but can be flexible.

---

13. Southern Baptist Convention, "Baptist Faith and Message, 2000," Statement of Faith, https://bfm.sbc.net/bfm2000/#vi-the-church (accessed January 21, 2022). The SBC's definition of church is included in Step Three, "Local Ministry: Establishing Healthy Churches," page 35.

In the Mallakani case study introduced at the beginning of this chapter, the sending church had not anticipated that decisions regarding the Smith's living location could be altered by the partnering agency that sponsored the couple's visa. Conflict arose because the agency made its decision without consulting the sending church. Although from the agency's perspective there was no other resolution, when the agency recognized that this decision-making authority was not specified in the partnership agreement, it could have chosen a more conciliatory course of action—such as taking the time to discuss the situation with the missionaries and the sending church. Without a prior agreement as to how these decisions would be determined, each entity made its own assumptions which, as it turned out, did not match. The unfortunate result was hurt feelings, conflict, discouraged missionaries, and most of all, an engaged people group losing its incarnational witness.

CULTURAL INFLUENCES ON PARTNERSHIPS

WITH THE ADVANTAGES THAT PARTNERSHIPS OFFER, what keeps these agreements from naturally taking place? Receptivity to forging partnership agreements can be influenced by the home culture of the sending church or agency. Many North American churches and agencies view the authority of the local church as paramount, as well as the responsibility to fully engage in the Missionary Task; they may not consider partnerships necessary. Other cultures, such as those in Latin America, are more accustomed to working in community and therefore often welcome partnering with others, but also expect a much more collaborative approach.

It is important to recognize differing cultural perspectives from the beginning because this understanding can help to clarify the expectations within the partnership. An example would be that North Americans tend to separate their work life from their social and family life, and therefore have a segmented view of how a multicultural missionary team might function. Other cultures, such as the Latin American culture, live life much more in community and would see a stronger blend between ministry life and personal life. A true partnership will require each colleague or entity to consider the needs of the other, embracing the requirements set out in Philippians 2:3, "Do nothing out of selfish ambition or conceit, but in humility consider others as more important than yourselves."

The Philippians passage should challenge all entities in a partnership—missionaries, churches, and agencies—to acknowledge the needs of others and the overarching task of making disciples of all nations, as commanded in the Great Commission. It is imperative that as partners working together discuss and adopt new structures and plans, the vision of establishing the church in places where there is no church remains the centerpiece of the endeavor. This is essentially keeping the vision focused on the effective implementation of the Missionary Task.

In the case of local churches that are independent in their approach to missions, their viewpoint may not be based so much on a conviction that they can "do it better," but that dependence on others is a surrendering of the autonomy that should belong to the local church. On the other hand, there are compelling examples of churches in the US cooperating for the sake of the Great Commission. Since 1925, the Cooperative Program within the Southern Baptist Convention has successfully pooled financial resources from thousands of churches to enhance missions sending. This cooperative approach encourages small as well as large churches to have a role in missions sending. While individual churches give up some strategy decisions and control to a trustee board that represents churches across the convention, the overall benefit is that churches do not have to have expertise in every aspect of missions sending and yet can participate in a missions-sending strategy with the goal of ensuring every unreached people and place will have access to the gospel.

CHALLENGES OF MISSIONARY LEADERSHIP AND SUPPORT

LIKE SOME LOCAL CHURCHES, missionaries also are independent spirits, a trait that is often necessary to function in challenging, isolated environments. They require empowerment and leadership, balanced with appropriate accountability and training. The Lord established the local church as his chosen structure for the fulfillment of the Great Commission. Few local churches, however, have the depth of expertise for every facet of missionary sending necessary in today's world. Therefore, local churches need to understand how to cooperate and trust the expertise of agencies and organizations that "do missions" on a full-time basis. These agencies have developed competence in the many unique security and cultural settings around the world, implementing appropriate strategies in each of those settings. In these cooperative agreements, the agencies, churches, teams on the mission field, and the missionaries should respect the perspectives of each of the entities and value the contributions of each to the missions enterprise. Most of all, it is important for the church to realize that kingdom resources should be channeled to take the gospel to those who have never heard. Agencies are often the only advocates for the vast populations of the unreached existing to this day.

As local churches understand the value of partnering with agencies in missions sending, agencies must recognize that without the local church, there is no missions effort; both missionaries and missionary support originate from within the local church. Furthermore, in this day of social media and instantaneous communication methods, the church is positioned to have an even more direct influence on the missions effort. Improved communications allow today's missionaries to look to their home churches for vision, encouragement, prayer support, and personal engagement in the task.

Field realities do not fit into any one structure and can change over time as a work develops and matures. What might have begun as the ministry of one missionary couple could end up as a combined effort involving several mission organizations from a number of countries and a growing national church. The decision-making and responsibility for that work will change with each step toward maturity and will hopefully lead to the national church taking on the full spectrum of responsibilities, thus becoming a healthy church ready to exit to partnership, embracing its own role in the Great Commission.

A PRODUCTIVE PARTNERSHIP

IN THE PHILIPPINES, five Baptist conventions are spread across the more than 7,000 islands of the archipelagic state. These separate conventions took shape during a time when communication and travel was difficult across the geographical divisions, and the conventions were formed to provide coordination and support for local churches in each region. The conventions, along with other Baptist organizations such as seminaries and the national Women's Missionary Union, have been interested in missions for years and had made a few successful attempts to send missionaries to other countries.

The conventions, however, discovered an existing channel through which they could radically ramp up their missions-sending efforts—a circumstance related to the Filipino economy that has provided an open door to take the gospel into all the world—even places difficult for Western missionaries to access. Because of high levels of unemployment in the Philippines, millions of Filipino workers leave their homeland annually for employment opportunities and higher wages elsewhere. These Filipinos often work as domestic laborers, such as nannies and cleaners, or as nurses or hospitality staff, among other jobs. Many of these jobs are in Asia or the Middle East. Thus, the churches and conventions in the Philippines found themselves in a unique situation to send missionaries not only through traditional church-supported means, but also via these overseas worker opportunities.

To coordinate these missions efforts, the five conventions partnered together to establish a missions agency called the One Sending Body (OSB). They agreed that the agency would lead in coordinating the sending of these "tentmaker" missionaries, including establishing missionary training programs and identifying strategic locations to place the workers. The conventions recognized the strength that would come from the five conventions and their churches partnering together in this effort—all for the sake of the Great Commission.

One of the seminaries volunteered its campus for a missionary training location. As the *Eight Steps* consultancy team, we led a workshop for

Filipino leaders and missionaries along with OSB board members, who then shared the *Eight Steps* consultation materials with pastors and church leaders in their various conventions. The conventions are now working together with OSB to identify where to send missionaries, how to strengthen their missionary assessment process, and the best ways to mobilize churches across the five conventions, helping them identify how they can get involved and contribute to the sending of cross-cultural missionaries from the Philippines.

LEARNING TO WORK TOGETHER

AS WE RETURN ONCE AGAIN to the situation of the Smiths working with the Mallakani people group, in the end, the missionaries, their sending church, and the missions-sending agency were able to talk through the situation, reconcile, and together they created a constructive path forward. In doing so, each party took time to clarify expectations for decision-making, and they defined a process for authority to be shared without hampering the work of the missionaries on the field. Additionally, the agency managed to solve the problem of platform leadership, and ultimately the Smiths were able to resume working among the Mallakani people. Even when conflict arises, the Bible provides a framework for resolving situations if all parties are willing to embrace the principles found in Matthew 18.

Working in a partnership is more than just cooperation between churches and agencies of one country and culture. It will become increasingly important in the years ahead for North American churches and agencies to partner with their counterparts from the majority world—a development that will bring challenges such as functioning well in a multicultural team setting. Different cultural perspectives can impact key issues such as decision making, accountability, leadership, and use of resources.

These cultural perspectives and nuances may influence a great number of areas. For example, majority world partners highly value relationships built on trust. North American partners highly value written agreements with the details of the partnership clearly spelled out and signed by both parties. When it comes to financial resources, too often majority world partners must sacrifice greatly to participate in missions efforts, while North American partners often participate out of a position of abundance. The measure should not be equal contribution, but rather equal sacrifice, whatever the contribution might be. Paternalism, dependency, sustainability, and reproducibility are all issues of consideration. Both North American and majority world partners must acknowledge the value each brings to the missions world and submit to one another in humility. With the bulk of evangelical missionaries now coming from the majority world, North American churches and agencies will have to discover what it means to be servant leaders as they relate to these partners and even perhaps redefine their own roles in missions sending. They may have to move to roles of facilitating, mentorship, and encouragement in addition to being on the front lines of engagement.[14]

Churches in many countries are discovering the strength of cooperative sending, learning how to navigate the challenges of authority, accountability, and cooperation. The maximization of our efforts means we must develop structures of mutual accountability and interdependence. This will require significant work from the outset but has the potential to reap much kingdom fruit as we determine how to walk forward, hand in hand, under the leadership of the Holy Spirit.

The Great Commission was given to all of Christ's churches, regardless of location and size. It is important that we recognize the value each brings to the task and nurture an attitude of service to one another as we work together to share the gospel with those who have never heard. This may be the greatest challenge for North American partners as they move from a position of control and authority to one of submitting to the leadership of our majority world partners.

Note: Material in this chapter is adapted from Carlton Vandagriff,* "Ongoing Relationships on the Mission Field," in *Whom Shall We Send? Understanding the Essentials of Sending Missionaries,* ed. Joel Sutton (Richmond, VA: IMB, 2016), 253-260.

14. Paul Borthwick discusses the themes of partnership, servanthood, and sacrifice in "Partnership Equality," in *Western Christians in Global Mission: What's the Role of the North American Church?* (Downers Grove, IL: InterVarsity Press, 2012), 149-156.

CONCLUSION

T HE WORLD'S POPULATION is approaching 8 billion souls. Governments are becoming more and more hostile to Christianity, and especially toward evangelicals who believe in the exclusivity of the gospel of Jesus Christ for salvation. At the writing of this book, more than 3,000 people groups remain unreached and unengaged with a gospel witness. The world's cities are growing exponentially with refugees, immigrants, and people seeking better lives, most of whom have had little exposure to the gospel of Jesus Christ. The Great Commission is a formidable task. How can we, the church, make a greater impact on lostness?

Beginning with Step Eight — "The Mission Field" — is critical to the process. Our efforts must point toward the effective implementation of the Missionary Task among unreached peoples and places. Although we quote the Great Commission from the final verses of Matthew 28 in most of our missions emphases, we sometimes neglect two key statements made by Jesus when he gave the command to his followers. The Great Commission begins with Jesus stating that, "All authority has been given to me in heaven and on earth" (Matthew 28:18). That is an immense statement. Not some authority, but all authority. That means he has dominion over all of this world in which we live. While on earth, he demonstrated this power by his miracles, not the least of which was calming the storm on the sea when the disciples feared they were all about to perish (Matthew 8:23-27). The disciples marveled that even the winds and sea obeyed him. Likewise, there are various types of turbulence surrounding our missions-sending efforts even to this day.

Christ's second key statement is how he concluded the Great Commission in Matthew: ". . . And remember, I am with you always, to the end of the age" (Matthew 28:20). This means he will never abandon us because the Holy Spirit, our helper, or Paraclete, has come alongside to help us (John 16:7). This should be an encouraging statement. The all-powerful Jesus, who has authority over all of creation, has promised to come alongside us and help us. All we are to do is to "make disciples of all nations ... teaching them to observe everything I have commanded you."

Sometimes we confuse our role in the process. One missionary, after a very difficult term on the field, stated, "I did not go to the mission field to not see fruit. I don't think I can continue if I don't see some results." Discouraging as a lack of results can be, each Christian has a significant contribution to make. In Romans 10:14-15, Paul asks: "And how can they hear without a preacher? And how can they preach unless they are sent?" So, the tasks of sending and preaching are critical to the process of evangelizing the world. Yet, we are not in control of the spiritual fruit. In 1 Corinthians 3:6, the apostle Paul acknowledges that while he planted the seeds of the gospel and Apollos watered those seeds, it was God who caused the growth. So it is with our efforts. We have a role to play, and we must be faithful in fulfilling that role as best we can. But any spiritual fruit we see comes from God and the supernatural working of his hand.

We had to challenge this discouraged missionary and his statement about requiring fruit. The challenge is that if God has called him to a place and a ministry, the missionary should embrace that calling, being obedient to follow the leading of the Holy Spirit. Whether or not there is fruit depends on the Lord. We are not responsible for the fruit, but we are responsible for being faithful to his call and being obedient to wherever he leads. It does not mean that we don't carefully evaluate our methods and strategies, but we are not in control of the fruit. We must leave that up to him.

Considering the huge task that remains to engage so many souls, we must recognize all of the resources God has provided for this task of making his name known among the nations. He is raising up his church around the world in all shapes and sizes: from the affluent North American church, to the persecuted church in Communist countries. Even churches in the poorest of nations are understanding God's call to be about his task. When churches read God's Word, the Holy Spirit will move them to be obedient to his task. As they step out in faith, God fulfills his promise by providing a way for them to fulfill his will. Seeing churches and agencies from impoverished countries or those shackled by oppressive governments still finding creative ways to send workers to the harvest should encourage us all. Truly, the vision of Matthew 24:14, "This good news of the kingdom will be proclaimed in all the world as a testimony to all nations, and then the end will come" is being fulfilled before our very eyes. God is about fulfilling his purpose. The church's role is to be obedient to fully embrace the calling he has given.

So, how do these *Eight Steps* help? It is important that we see our role in the Great Commission as a continuum. It is not just a simple task of sharing the gospel. The Missionary Task must involve the entire church and build a bridge from the local pastor and local church all the way to the mission field, with an intentionality to share the gospel with all the world. It encompasses all we do. We must focus all our efforts on establishing healthy multiplying churches among every people and place, so they can then fully embrace God's calling for them to be involved in the Great Commission.

This continuum will involve God's church from every part of the world. God is calling out his church, and his church is responding. The church must work together as one: the North American church cooperating with the South American church to accomplish the task. The African church must labor with the Asian church, and we can go on and on. Each local church will recognize its unique calling and be true to that calling, but we all have a role to play in equipping, facilitating, challenging, and cooperating in this massive task. All of God's church has a work to accomplish and we need each other to fulfill all God has called us to do.

The continuum is also about sustaining healthy missionaries on the field. We initiated the work of building the *Eight Steps* process to address the challenges of sustaining missionary presence. Incarnational witness is central to God's plan to share the gospel with the peoples of the world. As previously referenced from Romans 10, there must be a preacher (or proclaimer) and these individuals must be sent. This makes the sending and sustaining of missionaries a primary responsibility of the church.

It is not easy, nor is it simple. But it is the right thing to do. It is our prayer that a review and study of each of these *Eight Steps of the Missions Continuum* will assist and encourage churches, agencies, and missionaries from every part of the world to assess where they are now, identify concrete steps to advance the cause, and then take action to more fully embrace the calling God places on their hearts. In Isaiah 46:10, the prophet reflects on a promise of God that sustained the children of Israel during difficult times: ". . . my plan will take place, and I will do all my will." This should encourage every follower of Jesus because the victory will be won. Let's commit to work together in this awesome undertaking, recognizing that our Savior Jesus Christ has invited us to join him in the task of redeeming the world unto himself. There is no greater purpose.

Hal Cunnyngham, Ed.D.
Amanda Dimperio Davis, D.Min.

ABOUT THE AUTHORS

HAL CUNNYNGHAM, associate vice president for global engagement, has served with the International Mission Board for 37 years. He is responsible for diaspora missionary task strategies, global research, and globalization. He and his wife, Cynthia, served two years in Brazil as missionaries, followed by 23 years in East Asia. Field roles included church planting, administration, education, and church leadership training. In the US office, he led the IMB missionary personnel assessment and deployment process for eight years before assuming his current role.

Hal has a bachelor's degree in Agricultural Education and Biology, a master's degree in Educational Administration and Chemistry from Texas A&M Commerce, with a doctor of education degree in Educational Administration and Cognition from the University of North Texas. He also studied at Southwestern Baptist Theological Seminary and currently serves as an adjunct missions professor there. He is a contributing author of *Whom Shall We Send? Understanding the Essentials of Sending Missionaries,* a book which outlines the processes of raising up and sending cross-cultural missionaries.

The Cunnynghams have been married 46 years and have one son and two grandchildren.

AMANDA DIMPERIO DAVIS, director of globalization at the International Mission Board, has worked with the IMB for 20 years. As a single missionary, she served as a church planter and media missionary in Mexico, Bolivia, Peru, and Colombia. She graduated from the University of Alabama at Birmingham with a bachelor's degree in Mass Media and Broadcast Communications, and earned a master of divinity degree in Biblical Languages from Southwestern Baptist Theological Seminary.

Amanda is also an ASCP registered Medical Laboratory Scientist, having earned an associate of science degree. She recently earned a doctorate in ministry degree in Christian Leadership from Midwestern Baptist Theological Seminary. Amanda currently serves as an adjunct missions professor at SWBTS in both the English and Spanish programs.

She is married to D. Ray Davis, who also serves with the IMB.

APPENDIX

BIBLE STUDIES FOR CHURCH AND MISSIONARIES

LESSON 1

The Call to Missions

The call to cross-cultural missions is more than one simple event; it is a progression of "callings" that God makes to His servants. It is helpful to look at this calling in terms of seven targeted steps, with progression from point one of the target to point seven.

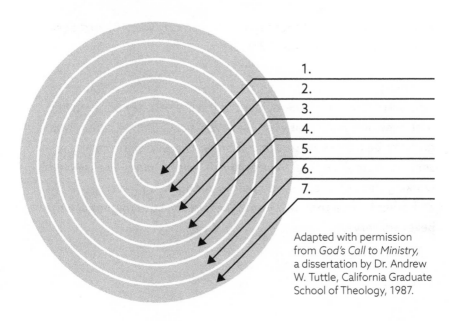

1. _____
2. _____
3. _____
4. _____
5. _____
6. _____
7. _____

Adapted with permission from *God's Call to Ministry,* a dissertation by Dr. Andrew W. Tuttle, California Graduate School of Theology, 1987.

1. Called to salvation in Jesus Christ (Romans 3:23, Romans 6:23, John 3:16-17, John 1:12), confirming they have responded in faith and repentance.

2. Called to the ministry of reconciliation, leading others to Christ (2 Corinthians 5:17-19).

3. Called to service in the local church (Romans 12:4, Romans 12:6-8, 1 Corinthians 12:4-6, 1 Corinthians 12:27-31).

4. Called to cross-cultural missions (Ephesians 4:11-12), answering the question: "Who is a Missionary?"

5. Called to take the gospel to the unreached, leaving home culture and family to cross cultural barriers for the sake of the gospel (Romans 10:11-15, John 20:21, Acts 1:8).

6. Affirmed by the local church (Romans 10:11-15, Acts 13:1-3).

7. Husband and wife together and in harmony with the expression of their calling (Ephesians 5:21-33).

Summary
The call of God should be evident in the life of every believer, but that does not mean that every believer is called to leave family and home to be a cross-cultural missionary. Therefore, the calling to serve as a cross-cultural missionary should be carefully assessed by working through these seven points, recognizing the stage of life and other factors that may impact where the Lord might have the believers serve.

Every believer is called in the following basic categories:

1. Call to Salvation
Responding to the Lord's expression of grace in faith and repentance.

2. Call to Mission
Essentially called to be a disciple of Christ and a disciple-maker.

3. Call to Station
Various stations of life require us to serve the Lord in terms of the realities of everyday life, such as being a parent, or maybe even being married or single.

4. Call to Service
God has endowed each believer with gifts to serve the local body of believers—the local church. These gifts are not all the same, but one should know one's spiritual gifts and use those gifts in service to the local church.

LESSON 2

The Command of Cross-Cultural Missions

ACTS 10

Part 1: God prepares Cornelius — Acts 10:1-8

Who is Cornelius? (vv 1-2)

How does God respond to Cornelius' prayer? (vv 3-6)

What did Cornelius do after his encounter with the angel? (vv 7-8)

Part 2: God prepares Peter — Acts 10:9-16

What do these verses tell us about Peter?

What was the problem with Peter eating the animals on the sheet?

Why did he see the same vision three times?

Part 3: Peter goes to see Cornelius in Caesarea — Acts 10:17-23

Peter senses the three men are from God and invites them to stay the night. (v 23)

Peter, along with some other believers, goes with the men on the next day. (v 23)

Cornelius worships Peter in error. (vv 25-26)

Cornelius and Peter explain their unusual experiences. (vv 28-33)

Part 4: Peter shares the gospel — Acts 10:34-43

Peter explains the new truth he just learned. (vv 34-35)

Peter shares about Jesus and that only through Him is there forgiveness of sin. (vv 35-43)

Part 5: The Holy Spirit confirms their conversion — Acts 10:44-48

The Holy Spirit comes upon them as a testimony to Peter and the others. (vv 44-46)

Peter determines that these new converts must be baptized. (v 47)

Peter stays there a few days, presumably to disciple these new believers. (v 48)

Conclusions

From Acts 10, what do we learn about cross-cultural missions?

From Acts 10, what do we learn about incarnational missions?

How does this chapter help you better prepare to minister cross-culturally?

LESSON 3

The Character of a Missionary

ROMANS 12:3-21

Review Romans 12:3-8.

In the church we are mutually dependent on each other, all functioning to build up the body of Christ.

Part A

Read verses 9-21. In the left column, write the commands we are to follow. In the right column, write the consequences of not following these commands.

Command to Follow	Consequences If We Fail
Example: *v 9 Love without hypocrisy*	*Show partiality in relationships*

Part B: Read Philippians 2:1-5

How does the discussion in Romans 12 compare with chapter 2:1-5 of Paul's letter to the Philippians?

How did Peter live out this principle in his interaction with Cornelius in Acts 10?

Reflect on your own life. Are there any areas where you might be tempted to neglect the teaching of Romans 12:9-21?

LESSON 4

The Life of a Missionary

MATTHEW 8:18-27

Introduction

Sometimes people view the life of a Christian worker as an exotic adventure where everything works out just as planned. On the contrary, following Jesus, especially in becoming a cross-cultural missionary, can lead to some challenging experiences. In Matthew 8:18-27, Jesus issued a call for people to follow him. Many expressed a willingness to do so, but Jesus' interactions with them tested their commitment and motivation. We need to ask ourselves the same questions today.

Part 1: The Scribe and Things Familiar — Matthew 8:18-20

How does Jesus' response to the scribe cause us to question the scribe's willingness to sacrifice?

What are some of the implications of Jesus' statement beyond just where one might live?

Are there comforts or luxuries in your own life that you might have a hard time giving up if the Lord calls you to serve in a different place?

Part 2: The Disciple and His Family — Matthew 8:21-22

Was the request of this disciple reasonable?

Why did Jesus give such a blunt response to the question?

How could following the call of Jesus impact your family relationships?

Part 3: The Disciples and the Storm — Matthew 8:23-27

Why were the disciples so surprised by the storm?

What did the disciples do that was correct?

Why did Jesus challenge their faith in verse 26?

What lesson was Jesus trying to teach the disciples through this experience?

LESSON 5

The Work of a Missionary

2 TIMOTHY 2:1-3; ACTS 18:18-27

Part 1: Paul's Instructions for Timothy — 2 Timothy 2:1-3

What is the foundation of Paul's strategy of establishing churches as he travels to unreached locations?

Part 2: Paul's Training of Aquila and Priscilla — Acts 18:18-27

What does the Scripture say? Briefly outline what happened in each section.

- Paul on the Move — v 18

- They arrive in Ephesus — vv 19-20

- Paul visits other locations — vv 22-23

- Aquila and Priscilla face a problem, Apollos — vv 24-26

- The result of their efforts — vv 27-28

Part 3: Paul's Strategy in Action

What is the relationship between Paul's instructions in 2 Timothy 2:2 and what he did in Acts 18:18-27?

What are some lessons or applications that missionaries might learn from Paul's instructions and actions?

What is the difference between the work of a local church pastor and the work of a cross-cultural missionary?